French Language
LIFELINES
for the Anglo
GENEALOGIST

French Language

LIFELINES

for the Anglo

GENEALOGIST

Tips and Tools for Tracking Your French-Canadian Ancestors

Sandra Goodwin

Goodwin
Genealogy
Productions

Portions of this text have appeared in podcast show notes postings by Sandra Goodwin on the Maple Stars and Stripes website at MapleStarsAndStripes.com.

Cover design: author

Publishing company logo: 777images

Printed in the United States of America

First Printing, 2020

ISBN 978-1-7351931-0-6

Library of Congress Control Number: 2020910728

Goodwin Genealogy Productions
P. O. Box 124
Leicester, Massachusetts 01524

To
Annette Marie (Sourdif) Goodwin,
Mom,
my inspiration for researching
my French-Canadian roots,
and my tireless mentor and assistant
during countless hours
memorizing high school
French vocabulary

Table of Contents

Table of Figures

Acknowledgments

There are several people to thank for the assistance they provided in getting this book ready for publication.

First, there's my honorary "editorial crew." To Margie Beldin, Ginny DeHaan, Pat McGrath, and Annette Smith, I couldn't have done it without you. Each brought a different level of French proficiency and genealogical expertise to the process and offered invaluable insights and suggestions.

A big thanks also goes out to the American-Canadian Genealogical Society for graciously sharing their file on French occupation words. That saved me from having to "reinvent the wheel."

I'm also very grateful to the Drouin Institute for access to and permission to use copies of their records. [Please note that sharing resources does not in any way imply that these organizations endorse this work.]

Introduction

When I was a kid, some might have thought I was a curious child. Others might have thought I was just plain nosy. I wanted to know what things meant. I would listen to adult conversations. If they were discussing something that I knew nothing about, I wanted to learn. When I watched a TV show or a movie, I hated when it was over my head. I hated that lost feeling. I wanted to know what was going on. I remember when I was in the third grade watching a movie about Antony and Cleopatra and not understanding the back story. Because of that, the movie didn't make sense to me. Perhaps that influenced my career track. I taught ancient history for several years.

I was also a voracious reader. There were many times when I'd come across a Spanish, French, or German word that was "like reading Greek." Out of the three languages, I found French to be the most perplexing. Words in French seemed to have the strangest letter combinations. I had no idea how to pronounce words with so many vowels! Take the Spanish word for "goodbye," *adios*. You don't need a Spanish lesson to produce a fairly accurate pronunciation. But *adieu*? Or *bateaux*? Or my favorite, *hors-d'œuvres*! That word was a real doozy and should be outlawed in

English-language texts! It wasn't until high school French class that I could pronounce and understand *that* word!

So I guess it was only natural that in high school I began taking foreign language classes as soon as I could. I took two years of Latin, three years of Spanish, and two years of French. Those foreign words were no longer going to get the better of me!

Then after four years of college, I graduated with a B. S. in education and a minor in teaching foreign languages.

Life Change

I ended my 35-year elementary teaching career without ever formally teaching a foreign language class. My skills became rusty. The only time I used my French was when I started researching my French-Canadian ancestry. Although I sometimes struggled, my friends constantly battled those mysterious documents. They could not read the valuable information locked up in those French records. They had never studied French and were at a distinct disadvantage. At least I had some basic knowledge to work with.

As I spent my last few pre-retirement years as a commuter, mp3 players became popular. Imagine holding an entire music collection on one small, portable device! Then along came something called a "podcast." Now I could listen to experts speak about topics I was actually interested in. My commute was fairly short, about eighteen miles round trip. It didn't matter. I thoroughly enjoyed my time in the car as I listened to one genealogy podcast after another. At some point I decided that after I retired, I would spend my golden years creating a podcast of my own. But what topic? Fifty percent of my ancestry was French-Canadian. I had spent many hours researching at French-Canadian libraries here in America. I had traveled to repositories in Quebec and Montreal. So I decided to try my hand at a French-Canadian genealogy podcast. *Maple Stars and Stripes: Your French-Canadian Genealogy Podcast*[1] was born.

---

[1] https://maplestarsandstripes.com

From a Seed, a Tree Grows

Feedback received from listeners indicated that one of the most helpful features of the podcast was the Language Tips. It helped non-French speakers understand some of the records and perhaps even break through a brick wall or two. But when you need answers, it's not always convenient to boot up the computer and hunt around in multiple episodes of audio podcasts looking for that one important piece of missing information.

So the idea for this book, *French Language Lifelines for the Anglo Genealogist*, was born. My hope is that you find the clues you need to better understand the records you collect. The more familiar you become with repeated words, the more stress-free your research will be. That is the goal: to enable you to quickly and accurately cull out details so you understand the type of document you're dealing with, the pertinent information in that document, and the next step in your research.

I also hope that this book aids in your search strategies. Finding French surnames in English records is a challenge. Often, the written French name sounds nothing like an English speaker would expect it to. If your French-Canadian ancestor said his name for a town clerk or census enumerator, there is no guarantee the name was written correctly. On the other hand, what exactly is a correct French spelling? One surname can be spelled ten, thirty, sometimes fifty or more different ways and still refer to the same family.

Where to Begin

Although it doesn't sound very exciting, I'd suggest you begin your linguistic adventure in the Appendix. Much of *French Language Lifelines...* is based on sounds, both English and French, and how differently the French language operates compared to English. I think *Appendix A: Language Review* will give you a solid introduction to concepts repeated throughout this book. Then, if you're looking for your ancestors in US census and vital records, try chapters 1–5 first. Use the chapters in Part 2 that correspond with the sounds in your ancestral surname. If you still can't find someone, delve deeper by using the *Search Strategy*

Toolkit in chapter 6. If you're trying to translate French baptism, marriage, or burial records in your possession, there's help in Part 4.

Online Tools

Throughout each chapter, I may refer to particular websites. To make these sites easier to access without having to hunt through each chapter, I've placed a list of each chapter's sites in a sidebar called *Online Tools*.

Even though these websites were checked immediately before publication, technology is constantly changing. Website URLs become outdated fairly quickly. I give you the complete URL for each site so that you can use the "parts" to hopefully pinpoint the new location. If a particular website brings up the dreaded 404 error message, try typing in the URL up to the first slash. Then do a search of the site for the particular article. Sometimes a redesigned website still has the page available, just under a new URL (website address). Also, look at the URL. If it begins with *http*, try typing *https* instead.

If that doesn't work, try doing a search for the topic. It may pop up if it's still available. Or, you might find some terrific new sites!

Hopefully, by using this book as a resource while you research, some of your obstacles will *poof*...disappear. Happy hunting, and may your journey be a bit smoother!

Part 1
Searching for
French-Canadian
Ancestors

Introduction to *Searching for French-Canadian Ancestors*

French surnames are certainly challenging. Sounds are different. Letter combinations are confusing. Spelling is constantly changing.

You cannot discover information on your family if you can't find them. Inability to locate a French-Canadian name in English-language records leads to many brick walls. To help you break down your wall, this section will demystify some of these roadblocks.

First we'll look at the names themselves. In chapter 1, I cover surname variations and *dit* names. Chapter 2 explains multiple given names, diminutives and pet names. The key to finding some surnames in online databases is knowing how to pronounce the word in French. In chapter 3, I present several methods for determining the correct pronunciation.

Next comes an explanation of the Soundex system for searching names with spelling variations. Then we look at using Soundex searches as well as other search algorithms to understand the strengths and weaknesses of each search strategy. This becomes more important every day as we move away from back-of-the-book indexes to online indexes.

Last, to make sure you've completed a search for every conceivable spelling variation, I've included a Search Strategy Toolkit which provides a systematic way of keeping track of which searches you've tried and which remain.

1
Surname Variations

My neighbor grew up believing she was English. She came from the Butler clan. "Butler" sounded very English, so she never questioned it.

My genealogical enthusiasm finally rubbed off on her. She decided to visit her 92-year-old aunt for a long overdue interview before it was too late. What a shock! My neighbor discovered that she wasn't English after all. She was French-Canadian! Her Bouthillette ancestors had changed their name to Butler.

They might have changed the name to make it easier for English speakers to spell or pronounce it. Or perhaps they did it so they could better fit in with their neighbors and not stand out as foreigners. This awareness of their name change was lost over time.

Working Backwards

All good genealogists conduct their research by working backwards. You will eventually come across the ancestors who were the first to migrate to the United States or another English-speaking region. Then you'll work your way back to a time when they lived in a French-speaking region. Research in each area has its own inherent set of challenges.

When our ancestors first emigrated from Quebec, Anglo town clerks and census enumerators butchered French surnames. It's important that you familiarize yourself with orthographic, or spelling, changes that occurred and evolved throughout the following decades. Also be on the lookout for other types of name changes and variations.

Eventually you'll discover the French surname your ancestor was using before the migration. The fun continues! You will very often find many (sometimes fifty or more) different ways to spell that surname in Quebec records.

To make your searches successful, it will help if you understand how various search engines work—for example, the difference between an exact search and a Soundex search (covered in ch. 4). Hunting for surname variations was a whole lot easier when we only had to run our fingers down a few columns in an index. Our eyes would scan and pick up possibilities. Now with online databases, you have to be craftier if you want to be successful.

Reasons for the Variations

There are many different reasons for French-Canadian surname variations. Understanding these reasons will help you determine if your ancestor is really missing from the record, or if you missed him or her in the index.

Immigration Challenges

There was a large influx of French-Canadians to the United States in the nineteenth century. Americans initially found French names very difficult to pronounce, so changes were made. Sometimes English-speaking clerks wrote what they heard. Sometimes our ancestors changed the name or spelling to better fit in with their neighbors.

Figure 1-1 shows examples of names changed based on their pronunciations.

Some French surnames are words with an exact English translation. The names in Figure 1-2 are examples of French names translated to their English meanings. In French, *la pierre* means "the stone." So an ancestor might use the English surname *Stone* or *Rock*.

Surnames: French to English Based on Pronunciation	
Benoit	Benway
Bouthilette	Butler
Cloutier	Cloukey
Mathieu	Micue
Ouillette	Willet
Pelletier	Peltier, Pelkey, Pelcher
Thibeault	Tebo

Figure 1-1: Surnames: French to English names based on pronunciation

If you are online, a quick check on the *Collins French Dictionary* website [2] will tell you if your surname (minus any initial *la*, *le*, or *l'*) translates directly to an English word.

In Quebec

Our ancestors also spelled their French surnames in a variety of ways even before moving to the United States. There were several reasons for this.

Surnames: French to English Based on Translation	
Lapierre	Stone, Rock
Roi	King
Lajeunesse	Young
L'Évesque	Bishop
L'Anglais	English
LeBlanc	White

Figure 1-2: Surnames: French to English names based on translation

Illiteracy was a factor until recent times. As in the United States, spelling was not consistent in the early days in Québec. Words were pronounced differently in different dialects. The priest wrote what he heard. If the speaker said *Leclerc*, the listener would hear /Leclair/. The listener might spell it exactly the way it sounded, *Leclair* or *Lecler*. If the speaker pronounced the final *c*, the listener might write *Leclerq*. There are several different letter combinations in French that make the same sound;

---

[2] https://www.collinsdictionary.com/dictionary/french-english

therefore, there are several different ways to spell a name that result in the same pronunciation.

Throughout New France's early history, battles were fought between the North American colonies whenever war broke out between England and France. Part of the military strategy on both sides was to take captives. When English captives were brought to Canada, many chose to stay, become French citizens, marry, and raise families.

Thus, English surnames were converted into French surnames based on pronunciation. Since many sounds are different or nonexistent in each language, creative spellings were abundant. The English names of captives were difficult to pronounce in French. Therefore, *Farnsworth* became *Phaneuf.* Captured members of the Otis family saw their name creatively spelled as *Hotesse, Autis*, and *Othis*.

Dit *Names*

To complicate matters even more, French-Canadians used *dit* names (see ch. 25). The word *dit* comes from the French word *dire*, which is the verb "to say." So when used in this context, it loosely translates to "called." Antoine Forget *dit* Latour is Antoine Forget *called* Latour.

The Why and the How

One question beginners often have is *why*. Why two different names in the first place? I have five different Pierre Pineaus in *my* database alone—fathers, sons, uncles, cousins. This was common in many families. So how does a family keep track of which Pierre they're talking about?

What if there were several Pierre Pineaus in one regiment in the army? How would people differentiate one from the other? They solved the problem by using *dit* names. In fact, a *nom de guerre*, as it was called, was required in early military days. A large number of *dit* names found in New France was a result of the Carignan Regiment, which was stationed there from 1665–1668. Many of these soldiers chose to stay behind when their regiment returned to France. They intermarried with locals and passed on their *dit* names. The most prolific *nom de guerre* is Lafleur, the *dit* name for over 200 different families.

How are *dit* names chosen (Figure 1-3)? A *dit* name could refer to the soldier's commanding officer, indicating which unit he was with. A *dit* name could also indicate a person's origins, as in *dit* Poitou, referring to someone who migrated from the French province of Poitou. If you wanted to distinguish a man with red hair from all others of the same name, you might call him *dit LeRoux. Roux* indicates red or auburn-colored hair.

Civilians used *dit* names also. In the early days of the colony, there was a limited number of surnames. A *dit* name could be used to distinguish two unrelated families who just happened to share the same last name and lived in the same region. On the other hand, if you've been doing your research for a while, you've no doubt discovered that large families were the norm. So a *dit* name could also be used to distinguish one branch of the family from the others.

One member of the family may have taken a *dit* name that referred to the area where he lived or to which he had relocated. An example is *dit LaRivière* for someone who lived near the river (as did just about everyone in New France). Sometimes the *dit* name came from an ancestor's name, like Robert, or from the name of an ancestor's land. Other times, the *dit* name gave a clue as to an ancestor's occupation, as in *Boulanger,* or "Baker" in English. Or perhaps the *dit* name evoked personality traits, like *dit LeSage* for a very wise ancestor.

Reasons for Dit Names
Nom de guerre (used by the military)
To distinguish between two unrelated families with the same surname
To distinguish different branches of the same family
To indicate place of origin
To indicate place of residence
To indicate a physical characteristic
To indicate a personality trait
To use the name of an ancestor
To indicate occupation

Figure 1-3: Reasons for *dit* names

How does all this affect your research? If you've run into a brick wall, you need to explore the possibility of a *dit* name. Perhaps you can't find an ancestor because he switched names!

Remember that *dit* names do not act the same way as surnames. Surnames were inherited by the children from their father. Originally a *dit* name could have been chosen, given, or assigned. Since *dit* names indicated origins, occupations, geographic locations, or physical characteristics, several totally unrelated people or families could use the same *dit* name.

Once a *dit* name was acquired, it was legal to use with or in place of the original surname. My ancestor, Antoine Forget *dit* Latour, was legally known as Antoine Forget, Antoine Latour, Antoine Forget *dit* Latour or even as Antoine Latour *dit* Forget, with the *dit* name taking the place of the surname. His children might use Forget *dit* Latour, or they might choose to go by Forget or Latour. You might find one brother in the records as Forget. The other brother might be listed as Latour. This could make it difficult to determine a relationship. Some lines could follow the Latour *dit* name for several generations. This resulted in descendants totally forgetting or no longer being aware that their ancestors started out as Forgets.

Women could also use *dite* names. Antoine's descendant, Denise, used Latour *dite* Forget in a majority of her records. (For more information on *dit* and *dite* names, see ch. 25.)

So if you're looking for a record for one of your ancestors, remember to check under both names. This is why a genealogist should record all surname variations for every person in their genealogy database.

Where to Find Lists of *Dit* Names

What if you don't know what a person's *dit* name might be? Where do you go to find out?

There are several resources available to French-Canadian researchers to help determine a possible *dit* name for a particular surname. Some surnames have only one *dit* name, and others have many. You may have to research all possibilities before you meet with success.

Books

Below you will find several books that list tables of surnames with *dit* names or other name variations. You can locate many available books in either **WorldCat**[3] or **Google Books**[4]. Some of these books are in French, but an English reader should be able to manage with very little trouble.

Répertoire des noms de famille du Québec, des origines à 1825 (which translates to *The Inventory of Quebec Family Names from the Beginning to 1825*) by Jetté and Lécuyer-This book also includes many Acadian family names. The text is in French, but it shouldn't be too difficult to find your way through the lists of names. This book is listed in Google Books with a publication date of 1988. It is still under copyright, so you will not be able to search that book from home. However, if you click on "Find in a library" and enter your zip code, you can find which nearby libraries carry it.

Jetté's book ***Dictionnaire généalogique des familles du Québec***-There is an index of surnames in the back of the book. The 1996 version includes corrections and additions. Again, a search in Google Books or WorldCat will indicate which nearby libraries have that book in its collection.

Index des surnoms et des sobriquets (Index of Family Nicknames) from the Archives nationales du Québec-You can find it on microfilm (film #6334281) or microfiche at the Family History Library and order a copy to be sent to a local family history center.

Volume seven of Tanguay's ***Dictionnaire généalogique des familles canadiennes***-This book is available in hard copy or online at the website of the *Bibliothèque et Archives Nationales du Québec*[5] (Figure 1-4).

---

[3] http://www.worldcat.org/
[4] http://books.google.com/
[5] http://numerique.banq.qc.ca/patrimoine/details/52327/2021541?docref=2GEer gOuOLTcwzyN4eM7cg

573			
N	NAVARE. Navarre. Navers.	NICANT. Comptois.	NOISEUX. Loiseux.
NADAL. Adal. St. Amour.	NAVERS. Navare.	NICOLAS. Delligne. Lavallée.	NOIZE. NOLAN (DE). Defosseneuve.
NADEAU. Belhair. Forcier. Grenier. Nadro. Lavigne.	NAVETIER. NÈCLE. Neste. NÉE. NÈGRE. NÉGRILLÉ.	NICOLE. LesBois. Nicolle. Vinière. NICOLET. Courval. DeBelleborne. Lubine. Poulin.	De la Marque. Lechevallier. Thierry. NOLAND. NOLET. Larivière. Passe-partout.
NADEREAU. Narderau. NADON. Létourneau. NADRO. Nadeau.	NEILSON. NEL. NELSON. Neilson. NELTIER.	NICOLLE. Nicole. NICOU.	NOLIN. Boncourage. Lafougère. NOM. NONPAREIL.

Figure 1-4: Example of *dit* names from Tanguay's *Dictionnaire généalogique des familles canadiennes*, volume 7

Robert Quintin's ***French Canadian Surnames: Aliases, Adulterations, and Anglicizations*-** It includes a mixture of *dit* names and other name variations (Figure 1-5). You can download this book from FamilySearch[6].

FRENCH-CANADIAN SURNAMES			
ALIASES, ADULTERATIONS AND ANGLICIZATIONS			
BEAUCERON	BEAUSSERON	BEAUNE	LAFRANCHISE
BEAUCHAMP	LAPRAIRIE	BEAUNE	RANCON
BEAUCHEMIN	LABRANCHE	BEAUNE	ST LOUIS
BEAUCHESNE	RACINE	BEAUPRE	BONHOMME
BEAUDE	BAUDE	BEAUREGARD	JARRED
BEAUDENESSE	ST JEAN	BEAUREGARD	JARRET
BEAUDET	BAUDET	BEAURIVAGE	RAGEOT
BEAUDET	DUCAP	BEAUSEJOUR	MARTEL
BEAUDET	LAMAY	BEAUSIER	TRANCHEMONTAGNE
BEAUDIN	BAUDIN	BEAUSOLEIL	DIAMEAUX
BEAUDIN	BODIN	BEAUVAIS	ST GEMME

Figure 1-5: *Dit* names from *French-Canadian Surnames: Aliases, Adulterations, and Anglicizations* by Robert Quintin

---

[6] https://www.familysearch.org/library/books/records/item/140015-redirection

Websites

There are websites that include compilations of *dit* names. The first is ***Family Names and Nicknames in Colonial Québec***[7]compiled by Father John L. Sullivan and Diane Paré Szabo (Figure 1-6).

NAME	SPELLING VARIATIONS	"DIT" NAMES
Abel	Abel, Abelle, Habel, Habele, Habelle	*Barbe, Benoit, Capel, Desjardins*
Abelin	Ablin, Ablain, Abelin, Ablin, Blain, Habelin, Hablin	*No dit names listed*
Abraham	Abraham,Abram, Abran, Habraham, Habran	*Cedula, Courville, Desmarais, Langevin, Pedrement*
Achee	Aché, Achée, Haché, Hachée, Harché, Harchey	*Chaveneau, Gallant, Hélot*
Achin	Achain, Achen, Achim, Achin,Haschin	*André, Baron, Bouteillier, St. Andre*

Figure 1-6: *Dit* names from *Family Names and Nicknames in Colonial Québec* by Fr. John L. Sullivan and Diane Paré Szabo, available online

Another is ***"dit" Names etc.***[8] compiled by the American-French Genealogical Society of Woonsocket, Rhode Island (Figure 1-7). You can also download a spreadsheet[9] of these names, allowing you to conduct a search for a particular surname throughout the entire document. The AFGS is also requesting additions to their list. If you have discovered any *dit* names in your research that are missing, there is a link to a Surname Variation Form that you can fill out and submit for inclusion on the AFGS website.

You can download a PDF copy of ***Patronymes et Noms Dits*** from the *Fédération québécoise des sociétés de généalogie* website[10].

On the **PRDH** website[11] ("PRDH" stands for the *Programme de Recherche en Démographie Historique du Québec*), you can type

---

[7] http://freepages.genealogy.rootsweb.ancestry.com/~unclefred/DitNames.html
[8] https://afgs.org/site/surname-variations/
[9] http://www.afgs.org/surnames.xls
[10] http://federationgenealogie.qc.ca/Fichiers/patronymes2.pdf
[11] http://www.genealogie.umontreal.ca/en/Stat/NomSurnom

in a name and get a list of *dit* names. Go to that site and type in any surname. You will clearly see why *dit* names cause brick walls.

Soulière	Lagiroflée		
Souligny	Leduc	Vinet	
Soulliard	Souilliard		
Soumande	Conanville	Delorme	DeL'Orme
Soumbrun			
Soumillier	Chamillier	Chomedey	Chomillier
Soumis	Saulnier	Saunier	
Soupiran	Mesin		
Soupras	Latouche		
Sourdif	Jourdif	Sourdive	Vadeboncoeur
Sourdive	Jourdine	Sourdif	Vadeboncoeur
Sourdy	Lamothe		
Sourin	DeBellecoste	Fournier	Lyverain
Souste			
Soutière	Lagiroflée		
Souvelin	Thouvenin		

Figure 1-7: From "dit" *Names etc.* by the American-French Genealogical Society, available online

Another page on the PRDH website [12] lists spelling variations found in the records.

So if you are stuck and can't get back any further on a particular line, make a list of alternative names for that surname. Then go back to the records from your ancestor's location. See if you can find him or her in those records under a different name.

---

[12] http://www.genealogy.umontreal.ca/en/Dico/Noms

Online Tools for Chapter 1

Collins French Dictionary (https://www.collinsdictionary.com/dictionary/french-english)

World Cat (http://www.worldcat.org/)

Google Books (http://books.google.com/)

Tanguay's *Dictionnaire généalogique des familles canadiennes*-click on volume 7 (http://numerique.banq.qc.ca/patrimoine/details/52327/2021541?docref=2GEergOuOLTcwzyN4eM7cg)

Quintin's **French Canadian Surnames: Aliases, Adulterations, and Anglicizations** (https://www.familysearch.org/library/books/records/item/140015-redirection)

Family Names and Nicknames in Colonial Québec compiled by Father John L. Sullivan and Diane Paré Szabo (http://freepages.genealogy.rootsweb.ancestry.com/~unclefred/DitNames.html)

"dit" Names etc. compiled by the American-French Genealogical Society (https://afgs.org/site/surname-variations/). To download a spreadsheet, go to (http://www.afgs.org/surnames.xls).

Patronymes et Noms Dits from the Fédération québécoise des sociétés de généalogie (http://federationgenealogie.qc.ca/Fichiers/patronymes2.pdf)

PRDH list of *dit* names (http://www.genealogie.umontreal.ca/en/Stat/NomSurnom) and surname variations (http://www.genealogy.umontreal.ca/en/Dico/Noms)

2
Given Names and Diminutives

Surnames are not the only problem you'll encounter with names. When a baby was born in Québec, he or she could be baptized with one, two, three, or even four given names. That person could use any of those names, or variations, in different records at different times in his or her life. That often makes it difficult to tell if you have the correct person or simply someone with the same name.

A baby's given names came from several different places.

❖ Parents could choose a name they like for their child, just as parents do today.

❖ Because of church influence, most boys had "Joseph" as one of their names; most girls had the given name of "Marie." This was, of course, in deference to Jesus's parents.

❖ Many times the parents honored a godfather or godmother by giving the child the godparent's name. Children could receive a name in honor of a deceased relative. That relative might be a deceased sibling or, occasionally, a parent's deceased former spouse.

* ❖ A baby could receive his or her name from a saint, especially the one on whose day the child was born.

* ❖ Boys could have a partial feminine name, such as Jean-Marie; girls could have a masculine name, such as Marie-Josèphte or Marie Josèphe.

French-Canadian Diminutives

Numbers alone are not the only problem. You also need to consider diminutives and pet names.

A diminutive can take the form of a name that, in appearance, does not seem to be related at all. When I was doing early New England research, I would often encounter a baby born with the name of Mary. While searching for her marriage, I might have a record where everything fit, except the bride's name was Polly. Were they the same person? On the surface, the names don't seem to be related at all. Yet "Polly" is a diminutive for "Mary." Some French names had similar alternatives.

Other diminutives add an affix[13], usually at the end of the name, that denotes smallness or familiarity. In English, an example would be "Tommy" for "Thomas."

Sometimes it can take beginning researchers a bit of practice to find their way around these not so diminutive challenges. It's as if the French were not about to be outdone by the English. They had to produce their own challenging names as well.

My maternal grandfather's name was Delphin Sourdif. Delphin is not a very common French-Canadian given name. I always wondered where the name came from. When I found his father Jule's naturalization record from 1884, it mentioned Jules's brother-in-law, Delphin Parent. Delphin provided Jule's character reference. Now I knew where my grandfather got his name. When I tried

---

[13] a prefix, infix, or suffix, added to a base or stem to form a fresh stem or a word

tracing Delphin Parent back into Canada, I couldn't find him. However, I did find someone who seemed to fit in every way except for the name. This person's name was Seraphin. Were Delphin and Seraphin the same person?

In chapter 7, I refer to my Collette ancestors. I mention that Etienne Collette and Sophie Brindamour had "between 17 and 19 children." Why don't I know the exact number? Because I'm still working out the possible use of multiple given names. Son Samuel also goes by the name Joachim and Anselme (at least, I think so). He was born Joachim in Ste-Hélène, but seemed to use Samuel here in America, switching every so often to the name Anselme. His brother Eliazim was born Onesime, but also uses Salim, and appears in two records as James (I think). Eliazim sounds like an Americanized version of Onesime, and Salim sounds like a diminutive. Those are the hypotheses I'm working on.

So if you want to know whether you are dealing with two different people or the same person who's using different names in different records, an understanding of diminutives could help.

Consider This

Here are some things to consider:

- ❖ Different diminutives were popular during different time periods. So Mariette for Marie was popular in the beginning of the 20th century, whereas Henriquet for Henri was popular several hundred years ago.

- ❖ Male names could have a feminine version with a diminutive ending, such as Etienne for a boy and Etiennette for a girl.

- ❖ Diminutive affixes indicated a nickname suggesting diminutive size. In English we would use Johnny in place of Little John. In French, Little Anne becomes Annette.

- ❖ Longer names were shortened to one or two syllables. Emmanuel or Emmanuelle might be shortened to Manu.

- ❖ Drop the first syllable and Christophe becomes Tophe.

- ❖ Double one syllable. Joseph becomes Jojo.

There are several diminutive affixes in French:

- ❖ *-et* (masculine)/*-ette* (feminine): Jacquet replaced Little Jacques. (The *t* does not sound because there is no final *e* at the end (see chapter 7). Little Jeanne would be Jeannette.

- ❖ *-ine*: An example is Michel for a boy and Micheline for a girl.

- ❖ *-elle*: Emmanuel for a boy; Emmanuelle for a girl.

- ❖ *-ot* (masculine)/*-otte* (feminine): Little Charles would become Charlot. The female version of Charles is Charlotte.

- ❖ Add the *-on* ending to a syllable from the given name: Antoinette became Toinon.

- ❖ *-ou*: Anne became Nanou.

- ❖ *-ick, -ic*: If your ancestor emigrated from Brittany, they might use the Breton ending *-ick* or *-ic*. So little Anne became Annick.

Male	Female
Alfonso	Alphonsine
Antoine	Antoinette
Bernard	Bernardette
Charles	Charlotte
Charles	Charline
Claude	Claudette
Etienne	Etiennette
François	Francette
François	Francine
George	Georgette
Georges	Georgine
Gillet	Gillette
Guillaume	Guillaumette
Guillaume	Guillemette
Henri	Henriette
Hugues	Huguette
Jacques	Jacquette
Jacques	Jacqueline
Jean	Jeannine
Joseph	Joséphine
Marcellus	Marcellette
Michel	Micheline
Modestus	Modestine
Odo	Odette
Paul	Paulette
Pierre	Pierrette
Pierre	Perrine
Pierre	Pierrick
Remi	Remiette
Thomas	Thomasse
Yves	Yvette

Figure 2-1: Feminine diminutives from masculine names

Figure 2-1 shows feminine diminutive versions of masculine names. Figure 2-2 shows both masculine and feminine diminutives formed from both male and female given names.

More Challenges

Even if a researcher is aware of all that, there are still challenges.

* ❖ People often used a different given name during different stages of their lives.
* ❖ Multiple children in a family used the same given name.
* ❖ Sometimes a name is hyphenated; sometimes it is not. You will see Marie-Madeleine as Marie Madeleine, Marie, or Madeleine.
* ❖ Sometimes priests wrote the register entries in Latin, so the researcher needs to be aware of the French equivalent of Latin names. (See Appendix J)
* ❖ In some records, names are abbreviated (for example, M-Jos.).
* ❖ Occasionally the original record is in poor shape or faded to the extent that it is very difficult to make out the letters. If the researcher is unfamiliar with French names, this makes it doubly difficult to decipher these words. (See Online Tools for Chapter 2 for websites with lists of given names. These resources might be helpful in pinpointing a difficult-to-read name.)

In the United States, given names could be Anglicized just as surnames were, making them difficult to trace in earlier records.

* ❖ Some stayed the same (ex: Paul, Joseph).
* ❖ Sometimes there were small spelling changes, facilitating the search (Olivier to Oliver; Edouard to Edward).
* ❖ Sometimes syllables were removed (Apolline to Pauline).
* ❖ Occasionally only initial consonants matched (Narcisse to Nelson).
* ❖ Some had similar sounds (Damase to Thomas).
* ❖ Some had no English equivalents (Toussaint, Théophile).

Name	Diminutive	Name	Diminutive
Adam	Adenet	**Denis**	Denisot
Adele	Adeline	**Didier**	Didou
Adeline	Aline	**Dominic**	Dimenche
Adeline	Aline	**Dominic**	Domin
Adeline	Deline	**Edmond**	Edmé
Agnés	Agnesot	**Éliane**	Liane
Alexandrine	Sandrine	**Élisabeth**	Lisette
Alice	Alison	**Élisabeth**	Lili
Alice	Alison	**Élisabeth**	Élise
All female names ending in -tine	Titine	**Élisabeth**	Lise
Amanda	Amandine	Elizabeth	Babette
André	Dédé	Emma	Emmet
Angela	Angeline	Emmanuel	Manu
Angèle	Angeline	Emmanu-elle	Manu
Anna	Anouk	**Estiene**	Thevenin
Anne	Annette	**Fabia**	Fabiola
Anne	Nanou	**Fleur**	Fleurette
Anne	Annick	**Flora**	Florette
Anne	Ninon	**Françoise**	Soizic
Annie	Nini	**Françoise**	France
Antoinette	Toinon	**Frederick**	Fred
Antoinette	Toinette	**Geneva**	Neva
Arnoul	Arnoulet	**Geneviève**	Ginette
Aubert	Aubertin	**Georgine**	Gigi
Augustin	Gus	**Gilberte**	Gilbertine
Augustin	Tintin	**Gilles**	Gillet
Bertha	Bertille	**Guillaume**	Guillaumet
Charles	Charlot	**Guillaume**	Guillemin
Charlotte	Lotte	**Guillaume**	Guillemot
Christine	Christelle	**Guy**	Guion
Christophe	Tophe	**Guy**	Guion
Christophe	Totophe	**Henri**	Henriquet
Claudia	Claudette	**Henri**	Riton
Claudia	Claudine	**Herleva**	Arlette
Clodovicus	Clovis	**Hugues**	Huguet

Name	Diminutive	Name	Diminutive
Jacques	Jacquet	Nicole	Nicolette
Jacques	Jaquin	Nicole	Nicoline
Jean	Jeannot	Nicolette	Colette
Jeanne	Jeannette	Nicolette	Colette
Jean-Phillippe	Jean-Phi	Nicoline	Coline
Joseph	Jojo	Nina	Ninette
Joséphine	Josette	Nina	Ninon
Joséphine	Fifi	Oda	Odette
Joséphine	Josiane	Odilia	Odette
Jules	Julot	Odo	Odilon
Julie	Juliette	Oudin	Oudinet
Julie	Juju	Paule	Paulette
Laura	Laurette	Philippe	Philou
Laura	Lorette	Philippe	Filou
Laure	Laurine	Philippe	Philippot
Laurens	Laurentin	Philippe	Philippin
Léon	Lionel	Pierre	Pierrot
Louis	Loulou	Pierre	Perrin
Louis	Louison	Ponce	Poncelet
Louis	Loïc	Ponce	Poncet
Louise	Louison	Raoul	Raoulet
Louise	Louisette	Raoul	Raoulin
Louise	Lilou	Raymon	Raymondin
Lucas	Luquin	Rogier	Rogerin
Lucie	Lucette	Roland	Rolet
Marguerite	Margot	Rose	Rosette
Marie	Mariette	Rose	Rosine
Marie	Marion	Sébastien	Bastien
Marie	Manon	Simon	Simonnet
Marie	Marielle	Théodore	Théo
Marie	Marise	Viola	Violette
Matilde	Tilde	Violet	Violette
Michel	Michelet	Virginie	Gigi
Nicolas	Colin	Yann	Yannick
Nicolas	Colet	Yann	Yannick

Figure 2-2: Diminutives formed from male and female given names

27

To solve a tricky research problem, you may find that you'll have to search under each of these names. Be sure to record all of them in your genealogy database.

Do you remember the laws of probability from junior high school math class? We can have up to four given names with all their diminutives and variations. Combine those with a possible twenty or more surname variations. The result is a staggering number of possible combinations. You might have to search many of these before experiencing success.[14]

So if you find yourself in a situation like this, understanding diminutives and name alternatives just might help you locate your missing relative in the records. A little determination and perseverance might help, too! (For help with given names, see Online Tools for Chapter 2.)

---

[14] See chapter 6 for a method to keep track of these variations.

Online Tools for Chapter 2

These resources may be helpful in determining a given name:

A list of compound given names at *Liste de prénoms composés français:* (https://everybody-wiki.com/Liste_de_prénoms_composés_français) These French names may not all be found in New France, but it's a place to start. Look for readable letter combinations in your record, and then conduct a search on this site.

A list of **French Name Days:** (https://www.be-hindthename.com/namedays/country/france) Check the saint for your ancestor's birthday. Some of these may have been carried over to Québec, especially in the early days.

The American-French Genealogical Society's web page **French-Canadian Given Names:** (https://homepages.rootsweb.com/~afgs/givenname.html)

Anglicized versions of given names. Male names are here: (https://en.wiktionary.org/wiki/Appendix:Translations_of_male_given_names_in_multiple_languages) Female names are here: (https://en.wiktionary.org/wiki/Appendix:Translations_of_female)

Acadian First Names: (http://www.acadian.org/first-names.html)

Common French male and female names are listed at **French-Canadian family trees:** Male: (http://frenchcanadianfamilytrees.blogspot.com/2008/08/prior-to-20th-century-most-french-boys.html) Females: (http://frenchcanadianfamilytrees.blogspot.com/2008/08/french-geneology-common-female-first.html)

The most common given names before 1800 from the **PRDH:** (https://www.prdh-igd.com/en/Palmares/TousLesPrenoms)

Louisiana Historic & Cultural Vistas's **French, Kouri-Vini, Spanish & English Diminutives of Given Names** (http://www.mylhcv.com/using-diminutives-given-names-identify-ancestors/)

Saints' names listed alphabetically: (https://www.be-hindthename.com/namesakes/list/saints/alpha)

3

Pronunciation and Text-to-Speech Aids

To be successful working in English-language records while searching for your French-Canadian ancestors, you have to take yourself back to when the record was generated. Think about the people involved. Who reported the information? Who recorded the information?

In many cases, especially in the early years of migration, someone with little or no knowledge of English, probably with a heavy accent, presented the information. The recording clerk probably knew no French and was shaking his head while this foreigner was pronouncing words with these strange, incomprehensible sounds.

And there are several sounds in French which have no corresponding sounds in English. So the clerk, upon hearing these sounds, interjected his own phonetic interpretation. This adds to the frustration of hunting for records that just aren't where you expect them to be.

Native Pronunciation is the Key

Understanding that hearing the native pronunciation can lead you to the misspelled foreign names in the records is the key. Listen, don't read. Listen to each syllable. Forget what's in front of your eyes. What do you hear?

Oh, that's right. You're not a native French speaker. So you have a predicament. You need to hear a name as if it were spoken by a native, but looking around, you're coming up short. What to do?

How do you locate a native pronunciation if there are no native French speakers left in your family? Here are several possibilities.

French Pronunciation

If you have the opportunity, ask a native French speaker. If no one in your immediate circle speaks French, here are some places to explore.

A local high school or college foreign language department

If the instructor is too busy to help on a regular basis, perhaps a second or third year student could lend occasional aid as part of the community service requirement. It might not be a "native" speaker, and high schools and colleges teach Parisian French, not Canadian French, but if that's all you have, take advantage of it.

A local French-Canadian genealogy society

If you are lucky enough to have a French-Canadian library or a genealogy society nearby with French-Canadian researchers, check there. There's nothing that brings back memories of childhood more than sitting in a French-Canadian library and listening to the old-timers (said with absolute respect and fondness!) speaking the language of your grandparents.

A local senior center

This works especially well if you live in an area that saw a large influx of French-Canadian immigrants back in the nineteenth century. Many of their descendants who grew up speaking French could be among the members of the senior center.

Social media sites like Facebook[15]

Again, someone might be willing to speak over Skype or send you an audio file to help you with the pronunciation.

Maple Stars and Stripes *Community Helpers*[16]

Members of the Maple Stars and Stripes podcast community volunteer to help with the French language.

Computerized Text-to-Speech Aids

Apps

Apps tend to come and go, so I am not going to list any particular ones here. To find an appropriate app, go into your device's store and search for a text-to-speech or a foreign language pronunciation app. Try to find one that actually pronounces Canadian French, such as *(How to) Pronounce PRO*.[17]

Websites

Oddcast's *Text-to-Speech* [18] : enter your name of interest, choose French as the language, then choose one of the Canadian voices.

Cepstral's We Build Voices[19]: In the Voice drop-down list, scroll down to Canadian-French and choose either the male or female voice. Type in your surname of interest. Then click "Say it."

Listen, then Write

Take the time to close your eyes and listen to the sounds. What do you hear? What would an English-speaking clerk have heard? Write what you hear phonetically, and search for that spelling.

---

[15] https://www.facebook.com/

[16] https://maplestarsandstripes.com/mss-community-helpers/

[17] https://itunes.apple.com/us/app/how-to-pronounce-pro/id953959208?mt=8

[18] http://www.oddcast.com/home/demos/tts/tts_example.php

[19] http://www.cepstral.com/en/demos

See chapter 6 for help in recording all possible spellings for each given surname.

Online Tools for Chapter 3

Facebook (https://www.facebook.com/)

Maple Stars and Stripes Community Helpers (https://maplestarsandstripes.com/mss-community-helpers/)

(How to) Pronounce PRO (https://itunes.apple.com/us/app/how-to-pronounce-pro/id953959208?mt=8)

Oddcast's **Text-to-Speech** (http://www.oddcast.com/home/demos/tts/tts_example.php)

Cepstral's We Build Voices (http://www.cepstral.com/en/demos)

4
Soundex Searches

Most genealogists would agree it is important to record all variations of a surname in your genealogy database. Others might disagree. They might feel it's not necessary because many database search functions include a Soundex search capability. But is that enough?

What Is the Soundex System?

Many of us old-timers remember cranking reel after reel of microfilm in the early days of our research. We remember using the Soundex/Miracode system for the 1910 US census. If your genealogy initiation began in the digital age, you may not know about the Soundex system. The US Census Bureau developed it in the 1920s to help index names in the census. Many immigrant groups like the Eastern Europeans had surnames with strange letter combinations. So did the French. Several of the different vowel combinations made the same sound. So the Soundex system grouped names together phonetically.

Each Soundex code consists of four characters. The first character is always the first letter of the surname, no matter whether it's a consonant or vowel. The next three digits are numbers based on consonants or consonant sounds. Vowels are ignored. Consonants from the same letter family that are formed in similar ways are grouped together and assigned the same number.

The number 1 is assigned to the consonants *b, f, p,* and *v* because /b/, /f/, /p/, and /v/ are phonetically similar (see Figure 4-1). The letters *c, g, j, k, q, s, x,* and *z* share a phonetic relationship, so they appear together in group 2. The sound of the /d/ and /t/ are similar, so the *d* and *t* are assigned the number 3. The letters *m* and *n* are similar and share the number 5. The letters *l* and *r* do not share characteristics with any other letter so are each assigned its own number, 4 and 6 respectively.

The letters *a, e, i, o, u, h, w,* and *y* are not coded. They are ignored except when they appear in the initial position. Apostrophes and hyphens are also omitted. Double letters are counted only once.

Let's see how we apply this when we're searching for an ancestor in an online database.

An Example

Let's take the surname Renaud. Where I grew up in New England, the name evolved to its phonetic spelling, *Reno*. Its Soundex code begins with the *R*, then the number five for the next consonant sound, which is the /n/. The last two digits would be zeroes since there are no more consonant

Letters	Phonetic Code
B, F, P, V	1
C, G, J, K, Q, S, X, Z	2
D, T	3
L	4
M, N	5
R	6
Vowels, H, W, Y, other characters like hyphens and apostrophes	Omitted

Figure 4-1: Soundex code system

sounds. So the Reno Soundex code is R500. This would cover such variations as Rano and Renou.

But the Soundex code for the surname Renaud, spelled the French way, would begin with the *R* followed by the number five for the letter *n*. Even though the *d* is silent (see chapter 7), English speakers creating the codes would not know that. So it would end with the number three for the *d*. The Soundex code for Renaud is R530.

Taking into account the various letter combinations that can be used to spell the surname Renaud (see chapter 9 on /ō/), there are no less than eight different Soundex codes for this one surname (see Figure 4-2). If you use the Soundex search function in any given database, and you type in only one of the many different ways the name can be spelled, that name will be assigned one particular Soundex code. That means you are eliminating the other seven Soundex codes with all the associated name variations. If your search results in 10,000 hits, the other seven Soundex results may appear later on. But how many of us actually check out all 10,000 hits.

In other words, if you rely on a Soundex search in an online database to locate all possible hits for your ancestor, and you type in Renaud, which is R530, you are missing at least twenty other candidates in seven different code groups.

The surname Hénault has a Soundex code of H543. Its variation, Heno, has a Soundex code of H500. But in French, the *H* is silent (see chapter 10); so the name actually begins with a vowel sound, most like the English /ā/ sound. So now we have to take into account the anglicized spellings Ano, with a code of A500, and Eno, E500.

Soundex codes would yield results as follows:

❖ Hénault = H543

❖ Heno = H500

❖ Ano = A500

❖ Eno = E500

List of eight corresponding Soundex codes for common spellings of the Renaud surname	
R253	Regnaud, Regnaut
R254	Regnault, Regneault
R500	Raineau, Rano, Reneau, Renno, Reno, Reyno, Renau
R520	Renaux, Reneaux, Renos
R523	Renost
R530	Rainaud, Renaud, Renaut, Renaust, Reneaut, Renot
R543	Renolds, Renauld, Renault, Reneault
R553	Renand (a misreading)

Figure 4-2: Soundex codes for Renaud surname

Would you like to give it a try? What are the Soundex codes for these names? (See Appendix C for answers.)

Tebo _____

Thibeault _____

Bauché _____

Boscher _____

Papineau _____

Papinot _____

Houde _____

Oude _____

Adhémar _____

Cadieux _____

Dallaire _____

Soundex Calculators

You don't have to figure out Soundex codes for every surname in your database! There's an easier way.

Most genealogy database programs have a built-in Soundex converter. Usually you'll find it under *Tools* on the menu bar. If you are looking for an online converter, try *YASC-Yet Another Soundex Converter*[20]. This utility allows you to convert several names at the same time. A search for *soundex converter* will bring up several others.

If you're having trouble finding your ancestors in an online database that uses a Soundex search, plug your various surnames into a Soundex converter. Make sure your online search consists of at least one name from each Soundex group. Chapters 5 and 6 expand this concept and demonstrate how to use the Soundex system to conduct thorough searches.

Online Tools for Chapter 4

YASC-Yet Another Soundex Converter–allows more than one Soundex conversion at one time (http://bradandkathy.com/genealogy/yasc.html)

---

[20] http://bradandkathy.com/genealogy/yasc.html

5
Understanding Search Engines

You're beginning your search for ancestors in the United States with the goal of moving back into Quebec documents. It is so important to locate every census and vital record associated with your ancestor for the duration of his or her time in the States. As a thorough researcher, you should also collect every census and vital record for extended family and associates (the FAN principle[21]). You never know which document will contain the name of the home village. Your ancestors may have been in the States for several generations. With multiple generations of large families, it's not uncommon to need to locate a hundred records or more per family.

---

[21] Elizabeth Shown Mills's method of researching a person's friends/family, associates, and neighbors; see https://www.evidenceexplained.com/content/quicklesson-11-identity-problems-fan-principle

A review of the records in your database will often expose gaps. Perhaps you found every census except for 1900. Perhaps you have an ancestor's birth and marriage record, but you haven't located his death record yet. You've tried different spellings of your ancestor's surname, but still no luck.

There are many terrific books explaining how to do thorough Google searches. Several deal specifically with genealogy, so there's no need for me to cover that here. This chapter deals with the particular issue of locating French names in English-language databases.

Search Algorithms

Let's look at the name *Thibeault.* It has nine letters but only four sounds, /t/, /ē/, /b/, /ō/. In this case, it takes several letters to make a few sounds. But there are also many cases when different letter combinations can make the same sound. This causes difficulty for English speakers, English-speaking clerks, and English-language search engines.

What do you do when you cannot locate an ancestor with a French surname in an online database? How do you know if the person wasn't in that geographical location at that time? Was he there, but the data collector missed him? Was he there, but you didn't find him? Was he wrongly indexed? Was he using a rare spelling of his surname? Did the clerk incorrectly write what he heard?

In this chapter, we'll learn about the different search algorithms used by three very popular English-language databases used for researching French-Canadian ancestors. In the following chapter, you can apply a basic understanding of how search engines work using various search parameters, including Soundex searches, to locate missing people. I'll give you a 4-step strategy. This tool will help you keep track of all surname variations so you don't miss *the one* your ancestor used in your impossible-to-find record. Following these steps will provide you with a complete surname list that will deny your ancestor the ability to hide behind that brick wall.

We'll begin by taking a look at how the search parameters work at Ancestry.com (a subscription site; free at some libraries). Then we'll discuss searching at FamilySearch.org, a free database used by many researchers. Many people can trace their French-Canadian ancestors back to New England, and approximately 900,000 of these immigrants came to Massachusetts. Therefore, I will also use the Massachusetts Vital Records database at americanancestors.org, the website of the New England Historic Genealogical Society (included with membership).

For the examples, I will conduct a search for an ancestor named Jean Baptiste Renaud. After each search, I'll compare the results so you gain an understanding of the strengths and weaknesses of each type of search. When you are facing a brick wall, one small shift in strategy might be all it takes to solve a longstanding problem.

Caveat: Websites change all the time. Even if these web pages have changed by the time this book is published, the concepts remain the same. It's always a good idea to take a few minutes to get the feel of a database's search function before diving in. This applies when you are researching *any* ancestor, but it is especially relevant when you're looking for a difficult-to-find ancestor.

Now let's look for our missing Jean-Baptiste Renaud in Ancestry.com, FamilySearch.org, and AmericanAncestors.org.

Ancestry.com

To demonstrate, I will begin my search with both the first name and last name boxes checked off for "Exact" search (Figure 5-1).

When I start typing in the name fields, the "Exact" choice appears. Click on "Exact" and other choices appear. By searching for the exact name *Jean Baptiste*, I am keeping the numbers smaller. I'm also isolating only the surname variations for this example. If I was really stuck and could not find him, I would, of course, want to search for variations of the given name such as J B, Jean B, Jn Bts, J Bte, John B, or John.

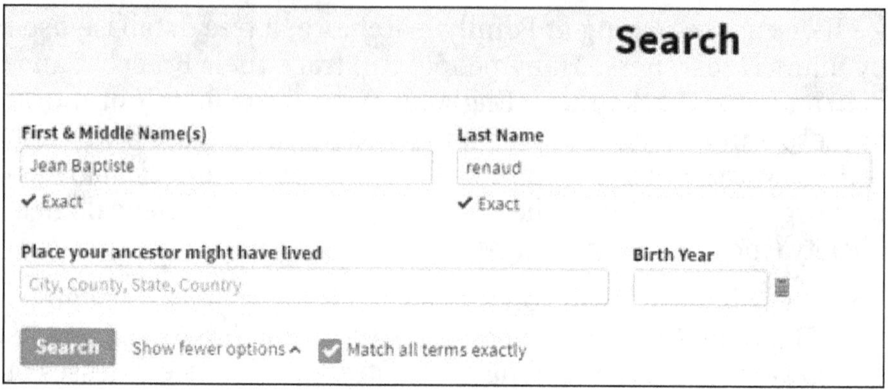

Figure 5-1: Ancestry.com *Exact* search

In the results (Figure 5-2), we'll focus on the *Wills, Probates, Land, Tax & Criminal* results.

In *Wills, Probates, Land, Tax & Criminal* (Figure 5-3), there are two results: *Slave Registers of former British Colonial dependencies, 1813–1834* and *US Social Security Applications and Claims Index, 1936–2007.*

If I go back to the search box and click on the word *Exact*, a drop-down box appears. In the second example, I've checked off *Exact* and *Sounds Like* (Figure 5-4).

I also receive two possibilities for *Wills, Probates, Land, Tax & Criminal.* These match the results in the first search.

In the third search, I check *Exact* and *Similar* (Figure 5-5).

I now have three results for *Wills, Probates, Land, Tax & Criminal* (Figure 5-6).

The extra category is *England & Wales, National Probate Calendar (Index of Wills and*

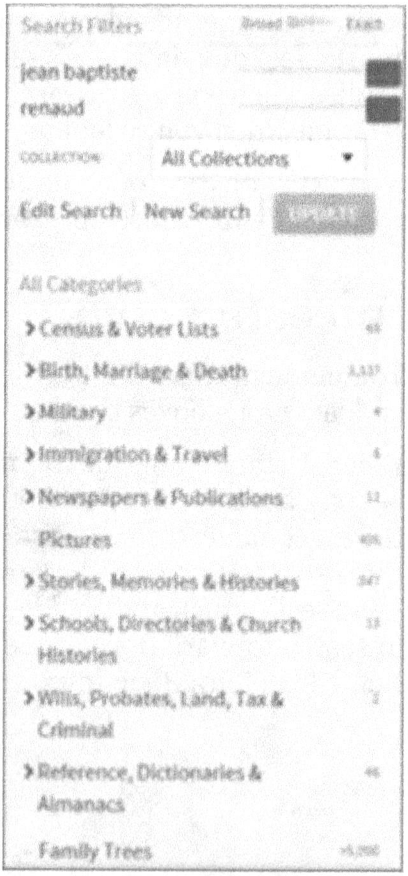

Figure 5-2: Search results

administrations), 1858–1966. In this case, the result is not what I'm looking for.

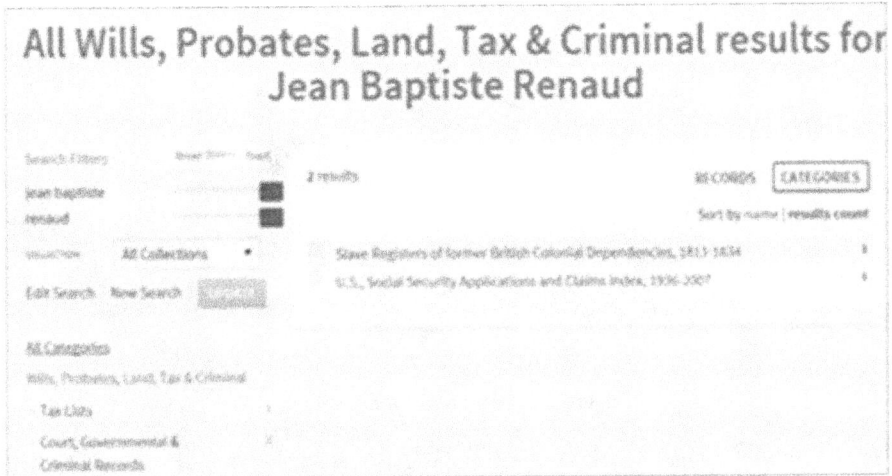

Figure 5-3: Two results show under *Wills, Probates, Land, Tax & Criminal*

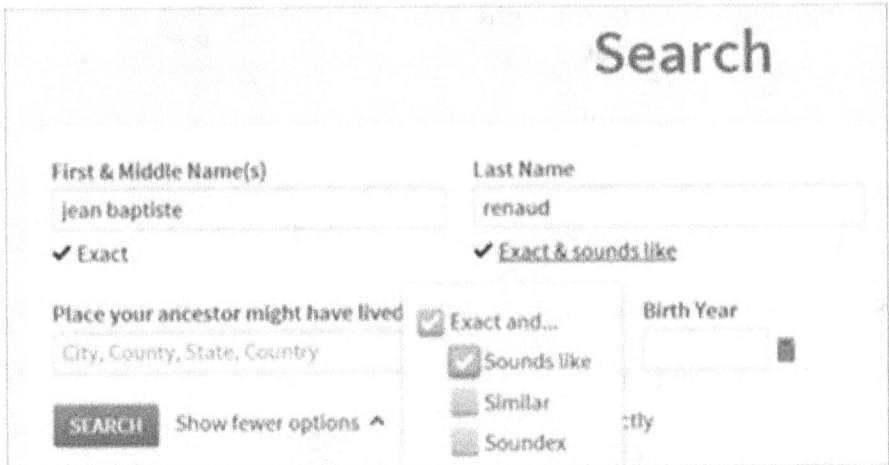

Figure 5-4: *Exact* and *Sounds like* search

My last search for Jean Baptiste Renaud is *Exact* and *Soundex* (Figure 5-7).

I now get ten results, the previous three as well as *US Patent and Trademark Office Patents, 1790–1909* and *England & Wales, Prerogative Court of Canterbury Wills, 1384–1858* (Figure 5-8).

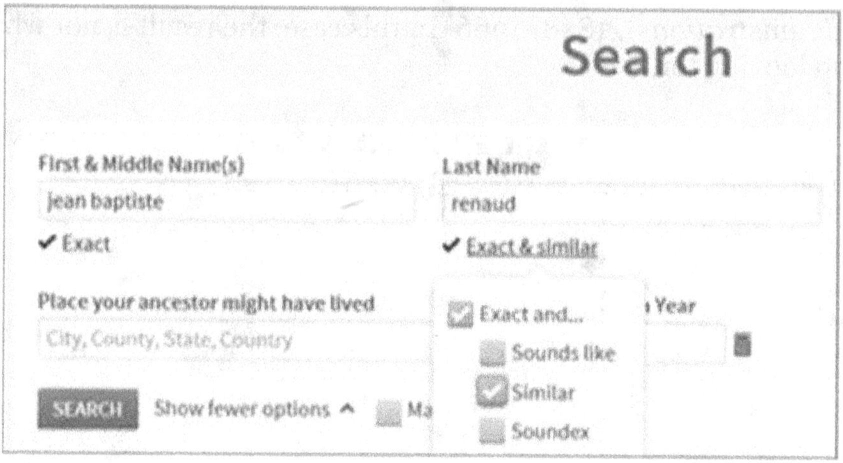

Figure 5-5: *Exact* and *Similar* search

In all cases, you receive more results with a Soundex search. Now, that may not be ideal when you are searching for a common name and receive 10,000+ results. But for a more uncommon surname, it might reveal possibilities that you hadn't encountered before.

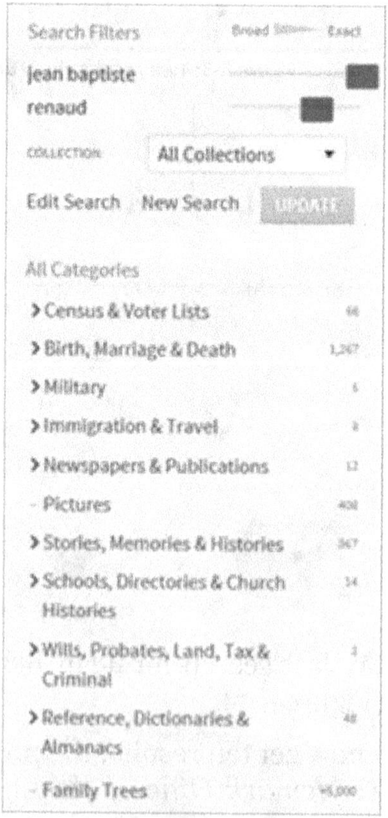

FamilySearch.org

When you are on the search page on familysearch.org, note the check box after the boxes for First Names and Last Names (Figure 5-9). When you check these, you are telling the search engine to bring up results that are an exact match. Let's see what we get for results using both methods.

In my first search for Jean Baptiste Renaud, I left the box unchecked. The result is 608,720 possibilities (Figure 5-10).

Figure 5-6: Results for *Exact* and *Similar* search

Notice that, in every result, the name is spelled r-e-n-a-u-d. This continues at one hundred results per page for over fifteen pages. On page 16, you will finally begin to see the surname spelled differently. However, these are not all Soundex matches (Figure 5-11).

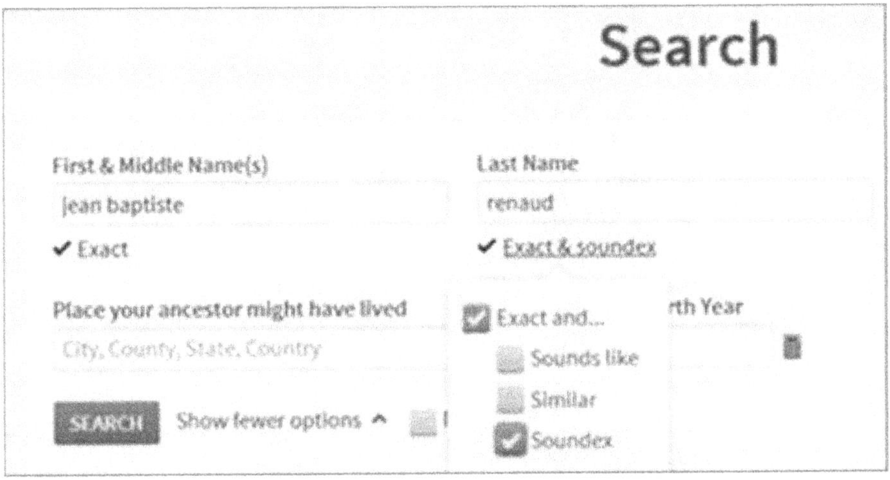

Figure 5-7: *Exact* and *Soundex* search

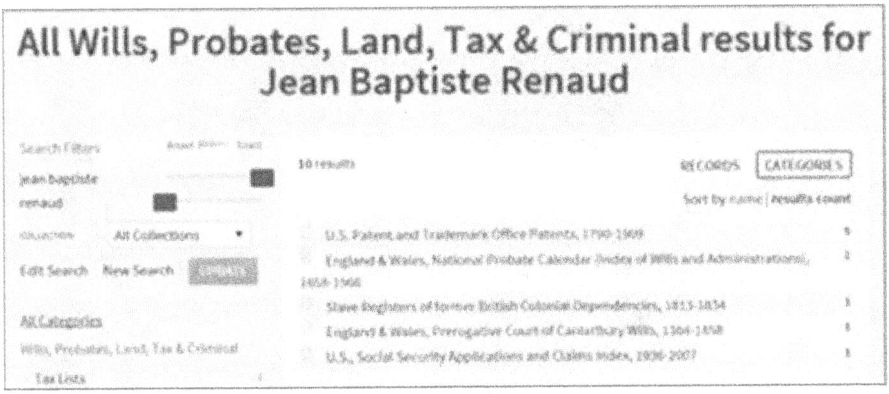

Figure 5-8: Results for *Exact* and *Soundex* search

Obviously, with so many results, you would want to include variations of the given name in your search parameters.

Now let's do an exact search on the surname only. To do this, check the box after the surname (Figure 5-12).We now have 28,059 results, all spelled r-e-n-a-u-d (Figure 5-13). Still a large amount, but additional filters should get that down to a more manageable number.

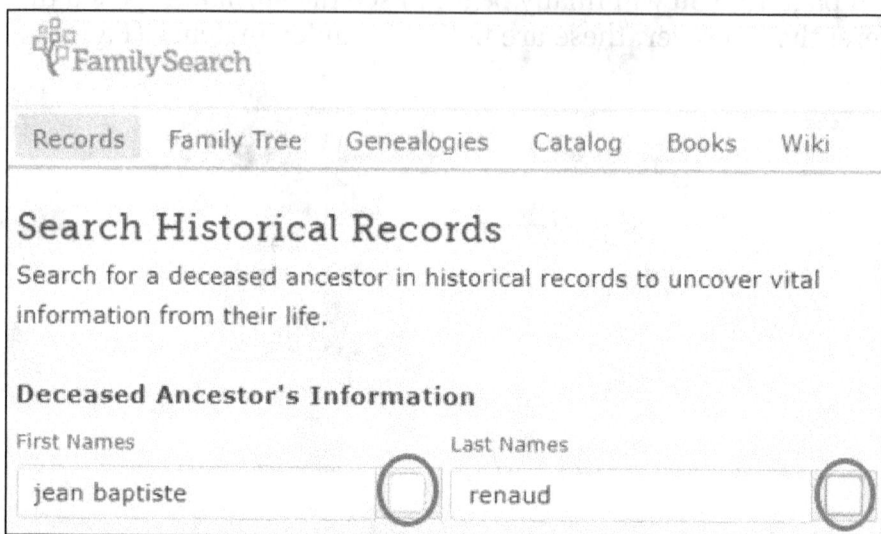

Figure 5-9: FamilySearch.org search box

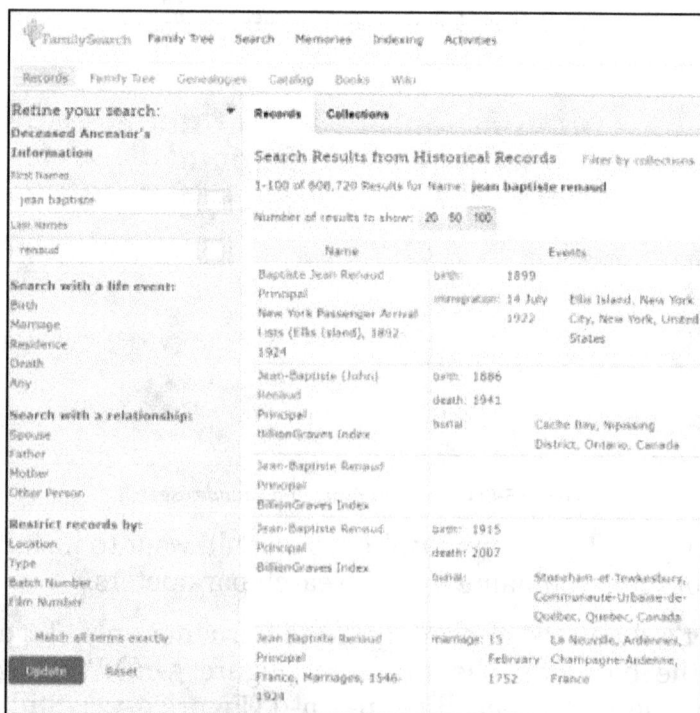

Figure 5-10: FamilySearch.org search results for Jean Baptiste Renaud

Jean Baptiste Renault
Principal
Quebec Births and Baptisms, 1662-1898

Jean Baptiste Renault
Principal
Quebec Births and Baptisms, 1662-1898

Jean Baptiste Renauld
Principal
Quebec Births and Baptisms, 1662-1898

Jean Baptiste Renauld
Principal
Quebec Births and Baptisms, 1662-1898

Jean Baptiste Juvinal Renault
Principal
Quebec Births and Baptisms, 1662-1898

Jean Baptiste Renault
Principal
Quebec Births and Baptisms, 1662-1898

Jean Baptiste Benoit Renault
Principal
Quebec Births and Baptisms, 1662-1898

Figure 5-11: Results, page 16

FamilySearch

Records   Family Tree   Genealogies   Catalog   Books   Wiki

Search Historical Records

Search for a deceased ancestor in historical records to uncover vital information from their life.

Deceased Ancestor's Information

First Names — jean baptiste
Last Names — renaud

Figure 5-12: FamilySearch.org Exact search

To apply filters, click on Refine your search (in the left side bar). You can now refine the search by collections, birthplace, birth year, marriage place, marriage year, residence place, residence year, death place, death year, other place, other year, or sex. Click on any of these, and you'll see a list of possible sub-filters. The

FamilySearch   Family Tree   Search   Memories   Indexing   Activities

Records   Family Tree   Genealogies   Catalog   Books   Wiki

Refine your search:
Deceased Ancestor's Information
First Names: jean baptiste
Last Names: renaud

Search with a life event:
Birth
Marriage
Residence
Death
Any

Search with a relationship:
Spouse
Father
Mother
Other Person

Restrict records by:
Location

Records   Collections

Search Results from Historical Records   Filter by collections

1,701-1,800 of 28,059 Results for Name: **jean baptiste renaud**

Number of results to show: 20 50 100

Name	Events	
Jean Renaud, Principal, France, Marriages, 1546-1924	marriage: 3 November 1757	Fraimbois, Meurthe-et-Moselle, Lorraine, France
Jean Polycarpe Renaud, Principal, France Deaths and Burials, 1546-1980	birth: 1735; death: 24 April 1811; burial: 25 April 1811; residence:	Bornay, Jura; Montmorot, Jura; Montmorot, Jura, Franche-Comté, France; Montmorot
Jean Xavier Renaud, Principal, France, Marriages, 1546-1924	birth: 1826; marriage: 5 February 1853	Reithouse, Jura, Franche-Comté, France

Figure 5-13: Results for Exact surname search

number at the end of each subcollection indicates how many records fit your new criteria.

If your ancestor is not showing up in these filtered searches, try expanding your results by eliminating some filters. For more tips on using filters in FamilySearch, go to https:// familysearch.org/blog/en/search-filt ers-familysearchorg/.

AmericanAncestors.org

If your ancestors resided in New England or the Northeast, you might consider joining the New England Historic Genealogical Society in Boston, Massachusetts. If you live too far to take advantage of their fabulous library, the *americanancestors.org* website contains many useful databases accessible to members from home. If you are not a member, try searching their indexes to see if any results look interesting. Then you can determine if it's worth your while to join.

There are two ways to search on websites with multiple databases: a general search of all databases or an in-depth search in one particular database. For a rare surname, a general search is a good place to start. However, when trying to find an ancestor in an individual database, search parameters often include those particular to that database and not found in the general search. This allows you to more readily navigate to positive results.

If I were searching for my ancestor in Massachusetts, I would use both the *Massachusetts Vital Records, 1841–1910* and the *Massachusetts Vital Records, 1911–1915* databases.

So let's conduct our search for Jean Baptiste Renaud in the first database, *Massachusetts Vital Records, 1841–1910*. (Click on "Search," "Browse Databases A–Z." In the "Search by Database Name," enter "Massachusetts." Then scroll down to Massachusetts Vital Records, 1841–1910.)

With *Jean Baptiste* as the first name and *Renaud* as the last name, I first checked the box *Exact Search* above the names (Figure 5-14). The search produced zero results.

For the Next search, I checked *Soundex* (Figure 5-15). That produced 949 results. One was indexed as *Jean B. Renaud*. Four

were for a John/Jean Renaud. The rest were all Soundex variations of the first or last name and not relevant.

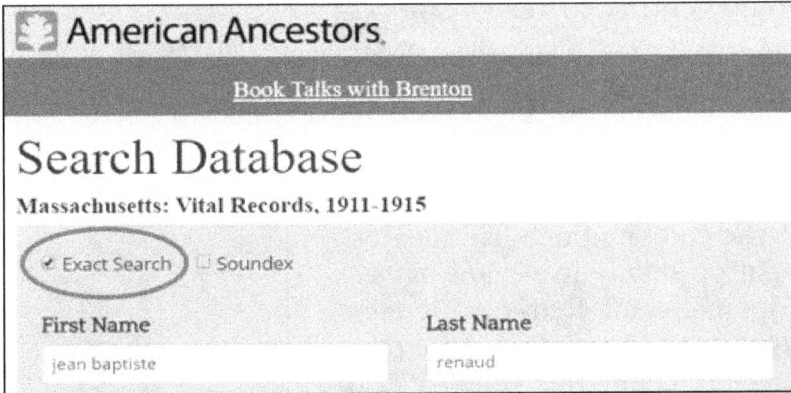

Figure 5-14: AmericanAncestors.org *Exact* search

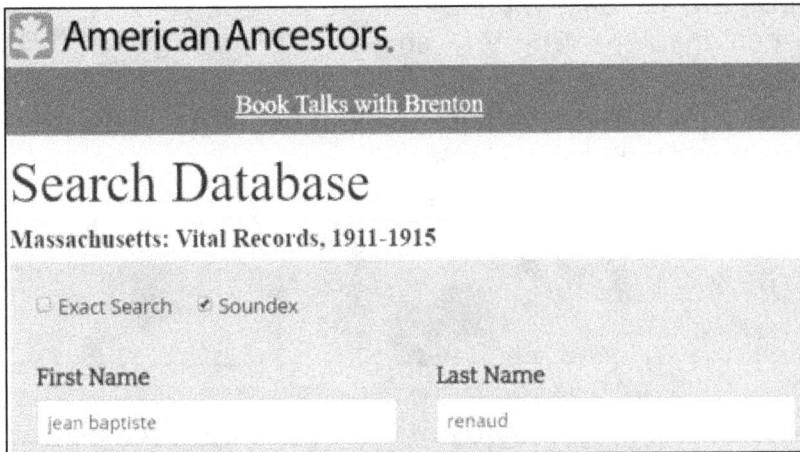

Figure 5-15: AmericanAncestors.org Soundex search

Wildcards

If available, try using wildcards in your searches. They can eliminate several steps for you by combining several searches in one.
This is particularly useful when researching French-Canadians
because of the multiple ways to spell the same sound.

For example, one of my family names, Boisjolie, can also be
spelled *Boisjoly* or *Boisjoli*. By searching for *Boisjol**, the asterisk
instructs the computer to search for the name with any

combination of one or more letters after Boisjol-. This brings up all three results in one search (Figure 5-16).

I can apply the same tactic with my Renaud search. By entering Ren* while also checking Soundex (Figure 5-17), I am telling the database to produce any records for names that begin with *Ren-* and conclude with any letter combinations. That search brought up totally irrelevant names like Rennell and Renwick. It also brought up my results from the previous search. But this time, it also brought up Jean B. Reno.

Besides the asterisk, you can use a question mark to replace a single character, such as *Re?naud.* That

Roland BOISJOLI
American Canadian Genealogical Society: Index of Baptisms, Marriages, and Burials, 1840-2000
Vital Records (incl. Bible, Cemetery, Church and SSDI)

Michael Joseph BOISJOLIE
American Canadian Genealogical Society: Index of Baptisms, Marriages, and Burials, 1840-2000
Vital Records (incl. Bible, Cemetery, Church and SSDI)

Joseph Amable BOISJOLY
American Canadian Genealogical Society: Index of Baptisms, Marriages, and Burials, 1840-2000
Vital Records (incl. Bible, Cemetery, Church and SSDI)

Figure 5-16: Search results using wildcard

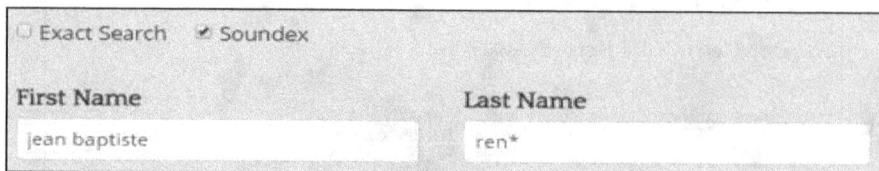

will not bring up a single Renaud, but it will bring up instances of Reynaud, Rennaud, Reanaud.

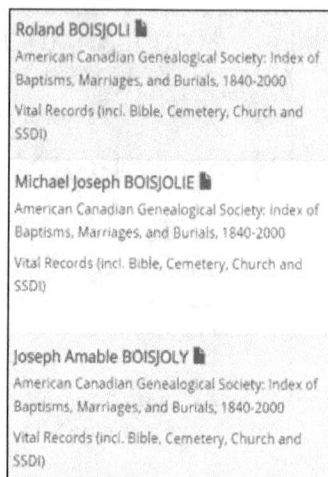

Exact Search   ☑ Soundex

First Name
jean baptiste

Last Name
ren*

Figure 5-17: Soundex search with wildcard

If you get nothing else from this chapter, I hope you now understand how important it is to take the time to understand how the searches work in any database you are using. If that ancestor is hiding, make sure he really *is* missing. You don't want a "lost" ancestor because you just didn't dig deeply enough.

In chapter 6, the Search Strategy Toolkit will provide a way for you to keep track of your surname searches. It's a systematic way to dig deeper until there is no place left to dig and no place left for those ancestors to hide.

Online Tools for Chapter 5

Elizabeth Shown Mills's **FAN Principle**- (https://www.evidenceex-plained.com/content/quicklesson-11-identity-problems-fan-princi-ple)

Ancestry.com- a subscription site; free at some libraries

FamilySearch.org- a free database used by many researchers

FamilySearch filters- (https://familysearch.org/blog/en/search-fil-ters-familysearchorg/)

AmericanAncestors.org- the website of the New England Historic Genealogical Society

6
The Search Strategy Toolkit

There are many times that you'll run into difficulty in the course of your research. Your ancestor should be in that census, but he's not. Your g-g-g-grandmother lived in a particular town her entire life. All her children lived in that town. Her death record should be there. But it's not!

Every so often we run into that disappearing ancestor. This toolkit will help you to use sounds, surnames, and Soundex to help you complete an exhaustive search for that ancestor. It's not designed for use with every surname in your family. Use it when you've tried everything else, and you want to make sure you have left no stone unturned.

Begin by making copies of Step 1: *Sounds Worksheet*; Step 2: *Surnames Worksheet*; and Step 3: *Soundex Worksheet* found in Appendix B. Then choose the surname of a stubborn ancestor who's hiding from you. Follow the steps below to make sure your searches are thorough. If you need a phonetic guide, see Appendix A. Good luck!

Step 1: Determine the Sounds in the Surname

Make a copy of the *Step 1: Sounds Worksheet* (Appendix B). I will use the surname *Renaud* as an example (Figure 6-1).

After *Search surname*, write the spelling of the surname that your ancestor used in his earliest US record. If your ancestor was a longtime resident of the United States by the time of your earliest record, look at his last pre-immigration Quebec record. If you have not yet traced your ancestor to Canada, use the earliest English spelling variation you have in your records.

If you do not know how this name was pronounced in Québec, do some research. Ask a French-speaking person or use an online text-to-speech app such as Oddcast's *Text-to-Speech*[22]. Try to use an app that includes an option for Canadian French. (See chapter 3.)

Write in your surname on the first line. Then close your eyes and listen to the sounds. Repeat it several times. On the worksheet after *Sounds in this surname*, write each individual consonant and vowel *sound* you hear.

RENAUD
= R
= Schwa sound (ə)
= N
= Long O

---

[22] http://www.oddcast.com/home/demos/tts/tts_example.php?sitepal; in Text-to-Speech, type your French name or phrase in the "Enter Text" box. Set "Language" for French. Under "Voice," use the drop down box to select one of the Canadian French choices, and click "Say It."

Step 1: *Sounds Worksheet* Example

Search surname:	Renaud	
Sounds in this surname:	R/e/n/aud = r ə n ō	
Sounds	**Letter combinations that make that sound**	
r	r, silent r	
ə	e, a, i, ey, ai, ay	
n	n, nn	
ō	au, aud, ault, aut, aux, auld, aulx, aul,	
	auls, aus, auts, eau, eaut, eaux, eault,	
	o, oe, olds, ow, ot, and [misspelling]	

Figure 6-1: Example: *Sounds Worksheet*

Phoneticists use an upside down *e* (ə) to indicate the schwa sound. So what exactly does that mean?

The schwa sound is the sound a vowel makes in an unstressed syllable. We often represent it as the /uh/ sound. Any vowel can produce the sound heard in an unstressed syllable. In *Renaud*, the stress is on the second syllable, so the first syllable vowel makes the sound /uh/.

Now write the individual sounds on the lines in the left column, one phonetic symbol per line.

In the right column, write every single way that sound can be spelled in French and English. Use Part 2 of this book, *Understanding Pronunciation*, to see if there is a chapter on a sound you need. For example, if your surname has a *d* in it, refer to chapter 16, *The Sound of /D/*. In the right column of your worksheet, include every variation found in the *Tips for Use with Search Strategy Toolkit* section for that chapter.

Be sure to check your genealogy database or notes for alternative spellings for your surname, such as Grumpy for Garriepy or Renand for Renaud. Be sure to include letters often confused by indexers or transcribers unfamiliar with the language (like *u* and *n* and capital *L* and *S*).

You could also look for alternative spellings on websites or in other sources which list surnames and variations, such as the following:

- ❖ Sullivan and Szabo's *Family Names and Nicknames in Colonial Québec*[23]

- ❖ *"dit" Names etc.* on the website of the American-French Genealogical Society[24]

- ❖ Robert Quintin's *The Dit Name: French Canadian Surnames: Aliases, Adulterations, and Anglicizations*[25]

- ❖ Tanguay's *Dictionnaire généalogique*, volume 7[26]

Find not only your surname, but other names with the same letter combination. Check the spelling variations. Did you miss any alternative spellings?

Be sure to include the way the sound is spelled in English also. You will be searching English-language records, after all, so it will help to know how an English speaker may have written that sound. For step 1, here is my list of all the sound variations I found for the surname Renaud.[27]

R	r, silent r (I have one instance of the surname written *Eno*)
schwa	e, a, i, ey, ai, ay
n	n, nn
long O	au, aud, auld, aul, aus, auls, aut, auts, ault, aux, aulx, eau, eaut, eaux, eault, o, oe, old, olds, ow, ot, and

---

[23] http://freepages.genealogy.rootsweb.ancestry.com/~unclefred/DitNames.html
[24] https://afgs.org/site/surname-variations/
[25] https://www.familysearch.org/library/books/records/item/140015-redirection
[26] http://numerique.banq.qc.ca/patrimoine/details/52327/2021541?docref=2GE ergOuOLTcwzyN4eM7cg
[27] Under "long O," I believe the "and" is a misreading of *aud*.

Once you have completed Step 1, you are now ready to determine all the possible spellings for that surname.

Step 2: Determine All Surname Variations

Now that you have a list of all spelling variations for each phonetic sound in your surname, it's now a matter of combining them. For this exercise, use *Step 2: Surnames Worksheet* (see Appendix B).

It is important to develop a system, or you will end up missing or repeating some combinations. Here's the system I use.

I begin with the first letter of the first three sounds, the *r*, *e*, and *n*. I then combine them with each variation for the long /ō/ sound. Using the *Surnames Worksheet* (Figure 6-2), I take the *r*, the *e* (first letter for the schwa sound), and the *n* and combine them with the *au* (first letter for the long /ō/ sound) to form *Renau*. This variation goes on the first line of the *Surname* column.

Continuing, I take the *r*, *e*, and *n* and combine them with the second spelling for the long /ō/ sound, *aud*, to form *Renaud*. This goes on the second line.

After completing all the sounds for long /ō/, I begin again. This time, however, I use the second letter for the schwa sound, the *a*. I then write the names *Ranau*, *Ranaud*, and so on until I complete all the sounds for long /ō/.

I then repeat the process by substituting the *i*, *ey*, *ai*, and *ay* in place of the schwa sound.

In the Soundex system, a single letter and a double letter receive the same code. So there is no need to redo each of these possibilities by substituting the *n* with *nn*.

Step 2: *Surnames Worksheet* Example

Surname variations: Write all possible combinations of a surname in the *Surname* column. In the *Soundex* column, write each

Surname	Soundex	Surname	Soundex
renau	R500	ranau	R500
renaud	R530	ranaud	R530
renault	R543	ranault	R543
renaut	R530	ranaut	R530
renaux	R520	ranaux	R520
renauld	R543	ranauld	R543
renaulx	R542	ranaulx	R542
renaul	R540	ranaul	R540
renauls	R542	ranauls	R542
renaus	R520	ranaus	R520
renauts	R532	ranauts	R532
reneau	R500	raneau	R500
reneaut	R530	raneaut	R530
reneaux	R520	raneaux	R520
reneault	R543	raneault	R543
reno	R500	rano	R500
renoe	R500	ranoe	R500
renolds	R543	ranolds	R543
renow	R500	ranow	R500
renot	R530	ranot	R530
renand	R553	ranand	R553

Figure 6-2: Example: *Surnames Worksheet*

surname's Soundex code. (This list is incomplete for the surname *Renaud*.) After substituting each letter that makes the schwa sound, I decided not to write out all the variations for the name when it was missing the initial *r* and began with an *e*. I have only ever found that in one instance of *Eno*. However, if I had exhausted all other possibilities, these would be other avenues to explore. I would replace the *R* with an *E*, leaving the three digits the same.

Once your lists are complete, use a Soundex converter to generate Soundex codes for each surname.[28] Place these codes in the Soundex column next to each name.

After writing the Soundex codes in the second column, you are now ready for Step 3.

Step 3: *Surnames Soundex Code*

Make a copy of *Step 3: Soundex Worksheet* (Appendix B). Go through your list of names from Step 2. Begin with the first Soundex code and write it on the top centered line in box 1. Now add all surnames with that code to that box (Figure 6-3). Check off each name on the Surnames Worksheet as you transfer it.

Go down the list and find the next Soundex code. Add all those surnames together in one box. Proceed down the list until you have grouped all surnames together with their codes. Use multiple boxes when needed.

Step 3: *Soundex Worksheet* Example

Group your surnames by Soundex code. Write one Soundex code at the top of each group. Then write all the surname variations that belong with each Soundex code. (Example below is a partial list only for the surname *Renaud*.)

Step 4: *Familiarize Yourself with Website Search Engines*

Most of my French-Canadian lines moved directly from Québec to Massachusetts. Therefore, I have scoured every census from several different sources for each family. I have also searched the Massachusetts Vital Records databases from the New England Historic Genealogical Society.[29] Each search engine is different.

---

[28] Many genealogy database programs have Soundex converters built in, or see the Online Tools for Chapter 4.
[29] https://www.americanancestors.org/index.aspx

R500	
renau	raneau
reneau	rano
reno	ranoe
renoe	ranow
renow	
ranau	

R530	
renaud	raneaut
renaut	ranot
reneaut	
renot	
ranaud	
ranaut	

R543	
renault	raneault
renauld	ranolds
reneault	
renolds	
ranault	
ranauld	

R520	
renaux	
reneaux	
ranaux	
raneaux	

Figure 6-3: Example: *Soundex Worksheet*

Now you are ready to put your sleuthing skills to good use.

Before working in these databases, take some time to experiment with the search engines. See how the different parameters affected the outcome. See chapter 5, Understanding Search Engines, for an explanation of how search engines work.

If a database uses a Soundex search, that's very helpful. However, you don't want to do just one search on one surname variation and move on. When conducting a Soundex search, be sure to use one name from *each box* on the *Soundex Worksheet*. Once you do that, the other names are automatically covered. This will ensure that you have included all possible spellings and pronunciations for that name.

Summary

In Part 2, Understanding Pronunciation, I cover the sounds of different letters. Use these various sounds in conjunction with the Search Strategy Toolkit to make an exhaustive search. It's important to know what sound a letter or letter combination makes in the Canadian French language. It's equally important to know how those letters would sound in the English language.

If I were looking for an ancestor with the surname Renaud, I would first search for the proper French pronunciation of the name. I would then write the sounds /r/, /ə/, /n/, and /ō/ on the Sounds Worksheet. Next, I would check chapter 9, The Sound of /Ō/, for different ways to spell the sound of long /ō/. I would include all the spelling variations on my Surnames Worksheet. Then I would group these by Soundex to make sure that I cover all codes when completing a search in any database.

Use this method for one of your brick walls, and perhaps it can help you finally solve your stubborn genealogical problem!

Online Tools for Chapter 6

Oddcast's **Text-to-Speech**-
(http://www.oddcast.com/home/demos/tts/tts_example.php?sitepal)

Sullivan and Szabo's **Family Names and Nicknames in Colonial Québec**- (http://freepages.genealogy.rootsweb.ancestry.com/~unclefred/DitNames.html)

"dit" **Names etc.** by the AFGS-
(https://afgs.org/site/surname-variations/)

Robert Quintin's **The *Dit* Name : French Canadian Surnames: Aliases, Adulterations, and Anglicizations**-
(https://www.familysearch.org/library/books/records/item/140015-redirection)

Tanguay's ***Dictionnaire généalogique*, volume 7**-
(http://numerique.banq.qc.ca/patrimoine/details/52327/2021541?docref=2GEergOuOLTcwzyN4eM7cg)

New England Historic Genealogical Society-
(https://www.americanancestors.org/index.aspx)

Part 2
Understanding
Pronunciation

Introduction to *Understanding Pronunciation*

Our French-Canadian ancestors moved to English-speaking areas and gave their names to clerks, lawyers, and enumerators. What these people heard did not always match what was intended.

When my aunt married my uncle and took on his very French-sounding surname, she got so tired of spelling it for people. The name included sounds that were not common in the English language. She tried pronouncing it so it sounded more English, but she still had to spell it.

So throughout history, if a clerk did not ask how to spell a name and just wrote what he heard, there was no telling what form that name took on paper.

On the other hand, let's say a Frenchman spelled his name for an Englishman. That Englishman then tried to pronounce it for someone else. There's no telling what that second person would hear and write. There were so many opportunities for misrepresentation.

The chapters in this section are intended to help you understand the sounds that the French letters make so you can figure out possible letter substitutions. It is necessary to know not only the French spellings and the French sounds, but also possible English spellings for those same sounds.

Included in the *Tip for Use with Search Strategy Toolkit* box at the end of each chapter is a summary of the information included in that chapter. Hopefully, this will make it easier to find without having to search through the chapter. Used in conjunction with the Search Strategy Toolkit in Chapter 6, you should be able to come up with a list of the most common surname variations.

7
Final Consonant, Silent *E*

I knew several Collette families in the small town in central Massachusetts where I grew up. In fact, my best friend through sixth grade was a Collette. Every Collette name I ever saw before I began my family's genealogy was spelled c-o-l-l-e-t-t-e.

One of the major premises in genealogy is that you start in the present and work backwards. As I worked my way back through the years and the generations, I was very surprised to discover that I also had Collette ancestors. The first family members I ran into spelled their surname the same way as my contemporaries did, c-o-l-l-e-t-t-e.

After researching back to approximately the 1870s or 1880s, I came across a different spelling, c-o-l-l-e-t-t. Further back, the name switched to c-o-l-l-e-t, a very common spelling in Québec.

My ancestors Etienne Collette and Sophie Brindamour had between 17 and 19 children. The reason I am not 100% sure is because some children went by more than one name.

In genealogy, we search out as much information as we can on our collateral lines, or the siblings of our ancestors, as well as our direct ancestral line. This not only makes for a better story, but it is often essential to plowing through your brick walls. For example, if your ancestor's vital records do not list his parents, perhaps one of his sibling's records will.

I researched all of Etienne and Sophie's many, many children. I worked backwards, finding their deaths, their children, their marriages, and their births. I found marriages for all of the children except for the oldest son Samuel. Massachusetts vital records are available online, so I checked all indexes in different databases. I could not find him even where he was supposed to be. But knowing the structure of the French language is what helped me eventually find success.

The Crucial Clue

In French pronunciation, you do not pronounce the final consonant of a word except when that word ends in one of the following consonants: C, R, F, or L. A way to remember this is that these are the consonants found in the word *careful*. (As in all languages, there are exceptions to this rule.) In order to hear the other consonants, you would place a silent *e* at the end.

Take, for example, my mother's name, *Annette*. You hear the /t/ sound at the end because of the silent *e* after it. On the other hand, think of how you pronounce the word *bouquet*. You do not hear the /t/ because there is no *e* after it.

So in America, my ancestor's name was spelled c-o-l-l-e-t-t-e and pronounced /Col-lette/. In Canada, where it was spelled c-o-l-l-e-t, the *t* was silent, and it was pronounced /Coll-ay/.

How does it sound? How would an English-speaking person think he should spell it?

I went back to the indexes and started searching for c-o-l-l-a-y. This is how it would have sounded to an American town clerk. I still didn't find him. However, I *was* successful when I altered that and looked for c-o-l-l-e-y. Samuel had gotten married eight short years after his family moved from Quebec to Massachusetts. He was still spelling his name the way it had been spelled in Quebec and pronouncing it /col-lay/ (Figure 7-1).

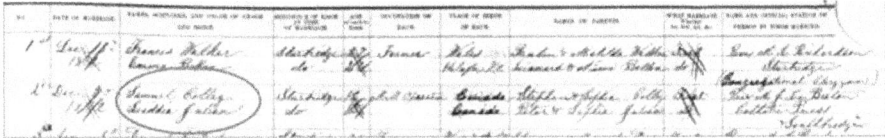

Figure 7-1: Marriage record for Samuel Colley (Collet), Mass. Vital Records vol. 255, page 322

Digitized Indexes

That is one of the problems with using digitized indexes. If I had been running my finger down the list of names in the index at the back of a book, my eye would've picked up *Samuel Colley* as a possible candidate for Samuel Collette. When you are using digitized indexes, however, you really have to consider every possible name variation (Figure 7-2). That is why, when you choose a genealogy database program, I highly recommend getting one that allows you to record every name variation, both first and last, that you discover in your ancestors' documents.

Hint: Always ask yourself, "How would an English-speaking person pronounce those letters?"

Vowel before the Consonant	Possible English Spellings
a (Cerrat, Dumat)	a, ah (Cerrah, Duma)
e (Vermet, Marsollet)	ay, ey (Vermey, Marsollay)
i (Gaborit, Petit)	ee, ie (Gaboree, Petie)
o (Ragot, Amelot)	o, oh (Ragoh, Amelo)
u (Chalut, Chaput)	oo, u (Chalu, Chapoo)

Figure 7-2: English spellings for French vowels

Tip for Use with Search Strategy Toolkit

For names ending in a consonant without a final *e*, the consonant will not sound (unless it's a *c, r, f, l,* or exception). Use the examples in Figure 7-2 to locate possible spellings for each vowel based on its pronunciation.

8
The Sound of /TH/

Genealogy is not for the faint of heart. Perseverance is a must. When you run into a problem, don't give up! New information or new methodologies will eventually lead you to a solution.

Ten-Year Search

Difficulty with the letters *th* created a ten-year search for my ancestors!

My maternal grandmother's name was Exina Mathieu. When I began my genealogical research on my mother's French-Canadian line, all I had was her baptismal certificate from St. Anne's Catholic Church in Fiskdale, Massachusetts. (Fiskdale is a village in the town of Sturbridge.) Written in French, it told me that she was baptized on November 21, 1896. It stated that her birth date was November 14, 1896 (Figure 8-1).

Very early in my research, I visited a Family History Center looking for information about my grandmother's birth. A patron there told me that the vital records from Sturbridge had burned in a fire. I mistakenly put off looking for that information for years. (Vital records were not available online at that time.)

Suggestion: Do not listen to well-intentioned fellow researchers without verifying what they say. That well-intentioned gentleman was incorrect; the vital records were available.

Figure 8-1: Baptism certificate for Exina Mathieu, St. Anne's Church, Fiskdale, MA, 21 Nov 1896

Several years later I visited the Sturbridge town clerk's office and looked for Exina's birth record from 1896. Not only was it not there, but there were no Mathieus in town at all until the 1950s.

So I thought, perhaps they lived in a surrounding town. Perhaps their town didn't have a Catholic church yet, so they had to travel to Fiskdale to attend St. Anne's. So I looked in the surrounding towns. In fact, over the next several years, I looked in all of Massachusetts and northeastern Connecticut. I found nothing.

So I went back to the baptism record. My grandmother's father was Alfred Mathieu. My mother vaguely remembered him. But listed as the godfather on the baptismal certificate was a man named Henry Mathieu, or *Henri* in French. No one knew who *he* was. Was he Alfred's brother? My mother and her siblings also remembered an Uncle Arthur Mathieu. So I set out to research all of them: Arthur, Henry, and Alfred.

I found Arthur's death certificate dated 1947. It gave his birthplace as Fiskdale, again part of the town of Sturbridge, the town that had no Mathieus in it until well into the twentieth century.

On Arthur's death certificate, it listed his father as George Mathieu, born in the town of Wauregan, Connecticut. I went to that town hall, and guess what? There were no signs of Mathieus born there either. Keep in mind that I was looking for any form of the word "Mathieu" that I could find. French spelling, English spelling; you name it, I looked for it.

I found my grandmother's brother's death record from 1957. Joe Mathieu was supposedly born in Sturbridge. But his birth record was not there either. I checked every census record that these people should have appeared in. Still nothing.

The Golden Obituary

Then I found George Mathieu's death record. George was my grandmother's grandfather. From that, I was able to retrieve his obituary. It confirmed that his sons were Fred, Henry, and Arthur. It also said that George was born in Putnam, Connecticut, a town with no record of any Mathieus. But I was really excited to learn the married names of three of his four sisters.

From the December 11, 1908, edition of the Worcester [MA] Daily Telegram, p. 9:

> "George Matthew, Formerly of Fisherville, Dies at Wilkonsonville"
>
> Died: December 10, 1908, Wilkinsonville, Massachusetts; aged 57 years, 3 months, 25 days
>
> Born: Putnam, Connecticut
>
> Married: over 30 years to Olive Collette
>
> Leaves: four sisters: Mrs. Marceline Obarton, Mrs. Sophrina Chauvin, Mrs. Josephine Jerin, Miss Alexina Matthew

The single sister Alexina appeared with her last name spelled M-a-t-t-h-e-w, an English spelling variation that I had already searched for unsuccessfully.

Since I was having no luck with the Mathieu surname, I decided to search for the three married sisters. Years went by. I always found Chauvin spelled the same way it was in the obituary. But "Jerin" turned out to be "Guerin," spelled in the records either *G-u-e-r-i-n* or *G-e-r-i-n*. Obarton remained a mystery. I had no idea what that last name really was for the longest time, and I never found it spelled that way again in any other records.

None of these searches helped me to solve the mystery of why my Mathieus were not showing up where they were supposed to be. I had searched several online databases. I had visited every town hall where they were supposed to be. I had checked the English spellings and the French spellings with one *t* or two *t*s. Not only did I not find *them*, I didn't find *any* Mathieus with that spelling, or close to that spelling, anywhere.

That Aha! Moment

Then one day I had one of those *Aha!* moments at the Connecticut State Library. You know the kind I mean. The kind where you shriek out loud even though you're in a library, and all your fellow genealogists seated near you smile in understanding.

I had decided to pursue the Chauvin sister, Sophronie Mathieu who had married Alphonse Chauvin, since that name was always spelled the same way. I conducted the search at the State Library because all the vital records are in one place. That saved me from having to drive from town hall to town hall. Here I could search in every town, spreading out in concentric circles. What I found was the birth of a son to Alphonso Chauvin and Sophronia *My-cue*![30]

When I got home after that research trip, I went immediately online to check the census records again. And there they all were,

---

[30] Plainfield, Connecticut, vital records, vol. 5, BMD 1867-1879 (part), roll #3277, p. 84, accessed at the Connecticut State Library

where they were supposed to be, but spelled M-y-c-u-e, M-i-c-u-e, and even M-a-c-a-e. Every census record and vital record was now easy to find. And then, in hindsight, it all made sense.

Family Birts and Dets

As a kid growing up, we spoke English in *my* household. But whenever I visited my grandmother, I would often hear my aunts and uncle, my great-aunts and my grandmother speaking French. When speaking to us kids, they would speak in English. I often wondered why they spoke a bit differently than we did. For example, they would say something like, "There have been several *birts* in the family this year," or "We only see my great-aunt at funerals when there's a *det* in the family." It was only when I took French class in high school that I understood.

In French, you *will* find the *th* letter combination, like in the surname Mathieu; however there is no /*th*/ sound as there is in English. It's an oversimplification to say it makes a /*t*/ sound. It's a softer sound than in English, made with the tongue closer to the back of the teeth. Think of pronouncing /*t*/ followed by /*s*/. This sound is not common in the English language.

The English pronunciation /Matthew/ becomes more like /Matchoo'/ in Canadian French. Even that's not precise. You really need to hear it.

If my ancestor walked into a New England town hall to apply for a marriage license and told the town clerk his or her name, it would have sounded more like /Ma-tchoo/. To an English-speaking town clerk, that more closely resembled /*Micue*/ than /*Matthew*/. Thus the spellings of M-y-c-u-e and M-i-c-u-e. Therefore, it helps to know the native pronunciation of a name in order to find the often incorrect spelling of that name (see ch 3).

This sound also applies to some names with a *ti*. So names like Pelletier, pronounced /pell'-tsee-ay/, show up in English records as Pelchey or Pelkey.

Oh, yes. The surname Obarton? That turned out to be the Anglicized spelling of Aubertin.

Hint: The Dictionary of Americanized French-Canadian Names: Onomastics and Genealogy *by Marc Picard had two of the spelling variations for Mathieu that would have saved me years of searching. Perhaps your surname clue is in there as well.*

Tip for Use with Search Strategy Toolkit

When looking for a difficult surname with a *th*, look for these other letters or combinations: *c, ch, d, k, qu, sh, t,* or *tt*. In a final syllable, you might also find an *-f* or *-tte*.

9
The Sound of /Ō/

Most genealogy database programs allow you to record name variations. Good genealogists know to record every single occurrence of a name for every ancestor. One of my ancestors, a Renaud, has thirty-eight different variations so far. One reason is because she was married four times. The other is because her birth name ends in /ō/.

Different Spellings for the Long O Sound

I descend from six different Renaud lines. The usual spelling for the immigrants' names was R-e-n-a-u-d. Most lines daughtered out early on.[31] But one line extends all the way down to my great-great-grandmother, Annie Josephine Renaud, born in 1848 in St-Pie. The name Renaud ends in /ō/. And sure enough, by the time

---

[31] "Daughtered out" means that there are no sons that procreate and pass on the surname to a surviving son.

the family makes it to twentieth-century Massachusetts, the name has evolved to *Reno*. Four sounds in the word; four letters. Nice and simple. But it wasn't always that way.

In my genealogy database, I have recorded no less than sixteen different ways to spell the surname Renaud, beginning with the *dit* name, Arnaud, and what I believe is a misspelling or a misreading of the written name, spelled r-e-n-a-n-d. I believe the last *n* was probably a misread *u*. The other fourteen are all spelling variations of the name. The names begin with the letters *rain-*, *ra-*, *regn-*, *ren-*, and *reyn-*. But the /ō/ at the end can be spelled *-aud*, *-auld*, *-aut*, *-ault*, *-eau*, *-eault*, *-o*, and *-olds*. If you're a mathematician and you're good with probability, you can probably figure out how many different name combinations we can get with five different first syllables and eight different last syllables. Here are the most common in my database:

Rainaud	Raineau	Rano	Ranolds	Regneault
Renaud	Renauld	Renault	Renaut	Reneau
Reneault	Renno	Reno	Reyno	

On top of that, when I went into my database and found other surnames that ended in the /ō/, I came up with nine other ways to spell that sound. One of them is an *-ow*, and it is found in an American record, so it's not really a French spelling. But the other eight are *-au*, *-aust*, *-aux*, *-eaut*, *-eaux*, *-os*, *-ost*, and *-ot*. That's a grand total of sixteen different letter combinations for the /ō/ found at the end of surnames like Renaud, Pineau, and Buteau.

Other ways of spelling the /ō/:

-au	-aust	-aux	-eaut
-eaux	-os	-ost	-ot

Why are there so many different combinations? If you've read Chapter 7, we discussed that you do not pronounce the final consonant of a word unless there is a silent *e* at the end. That means once you reach your final vowel or vowel combination in a word, it doesn't matter what consonants you stick on the end. You're not going to hear them anyhow. So if you go up to the priest and tell him your name is Provo, he might spell it P-r-o-v-o, or he might add a *t* or an *st* to the end. It's still pronounced the same way.

Some online indexes allow Soundex searches. The Soundex system groups names phonetically rather than alphabetically. See chapter 4 for examples of Soundex codes using the Renaud surname.

Tip for Use with Search Strategy Toolkit

There are many different letter combinations that make the /ō/ in French:

au, aud, ault, aut, aux, auld, aulx, aul, auls, aus, auts, eau, eaud, eaut, eaux, eault, o, olds, olt, os, and *ot.*

When searching in English-language records, you must also remember the English letter combinations that might spell the /ō/ in French names:

o + consonant + silent *e, ow, owe, oa, oe, O'-, Ho.*

As a last resort, check out these spellings. They are not truly spellings for the /ō/, yet, depending on dialect, you might see these in some cases:

aw, eu, on, ou, oue, oux, and *u.*

10
The Mute *H*

In the French language, the letter *h* is known as a mute *h*. That means that it does not make the /*h*/ sound as in English. When it is the first letter of a word, the word starts with the following vowel sound. So what does this have to do with genealogy?

Let's look at the surname Hénault. Perhaps your Hénault line extends for generations, long enough to have migrated to America or another English-speaking part of the world a century or more ago. Was there a spelling change in those intervening years? At some point, you can no longer find them in the records. Close your eyes and listen to the sounds. In French, you only hear three sounds, the long *a*, the *n*, and the long *o*. What are some ways that an English speaking person would spell it? *Ano* is an obvious one. I have also found the name spelled *Eno*.

The same also applies to the surname Hunault. How does that sound? Yes, you can occasionally find it spelled *Uno*.

Let's say you're researching from the present and going back through the generations. One of your French-Canadian ancestors marries someone whose name starts with a vowel, like *Ano*. You can't seem to get back any further. Try looking for the name spelled with either an *h* or another vowel like *e*, because the French *é* (with the accent aigu) approximates the long *a* sound.

Look at one of the following resources that lists name variations. You'll find the URLs for these in *Online Tools for Chapter 1*:

❖ Robert Quintin's *French Canadian Surnames: Aliases, Adulterations, and Anglicizations*

❖ Sullivan and Szabo's *Family Names and Nicknames in Colonial Québec* website

❖ "dit" *Names etc.* compiled by the American-French Genealogical Society.

Look through the surnames beginning with the letter *h* and the ones beginning with vowels to get an idea of the many different ways to spell these sounds.

If my American ancestors spelled their name *Ano*, and I was trying to figure out other ways to spell it, I could go, for example, to the **Family Names and Nicknames in Colonial Québec** website and look up *Ano*. I would discover that it isn't there. But if I glance through the surnames that begin with *a*, and remember what I know about all the different spellings for the long *o* sound, I would recognize that *Aineau* is the same sounding name as *Ano*. Here you will find fifteen different spellings alphabetized under three different initial letters (Figure 10-1).

Aineau	Aineau, Enau, Enaud, Eneau, Eneaud, Eno, Enos, Esnaud, Esneault, Hainau, Henau, Heneault, Heneaut, Heno, Henot

Figure 10-1: Various spellings for the surname Aineau, from Sullivan and Szabo's *Family Names and Nicknames in Colonial Québec*

An interesting story is that of the Otis family. In 1689, Indians attacked Dover, New Hampshire, in what is known as the Cocheco Massacre. Richard Otis and a daughter were killed. His wife and another daughter Margaret, a baby at the time, were taken captive and brought back to Canada. The priests took the baby and renamed her Christine. She was raised by the nuns, and at the age of eighteen married Louis Lebeau, the brother of one of my ancestors. In her marriage record dated June 14, 1707, her name is spelled *Otesse*, whereas her father's name in the same record is spelled *Hautesse*.

In the *Family Names and Nicknames in Colonial Québec* website, you will find the name Otis spelled seven different ways with three different initial letters (Figure 10-2).

Otis	Autis, Hotesse, Hotisse, Otheis, Othis, Otice, Otisse

Figure 10-2: Various spellings for the surname Otis, from Sullivan and Szabo's *Family Names and Nicknames in Colonial Québec*

Remember that some names that begin with the mute *h* may be spelled with different beginning vowel combinations. You need to look for all of them.

Hint: When you are dealing with a surname with an initial h, look also for names beginning with vowels. If the name begins with a vowel, search for that word with a beginning h or a different vowel.

Tip for Use with Search Strategy Toolkit

For surnames beginning with the letter *h*, look for that name beginning with a vowel.

For surnames beginning with the letter *a*, look for that name beginning with *h* or *e*.

For surnames beginning with the letter *e*, look for that name beginning with *a* or *h*.

For surnames with more than one syllable beginning with the letter *h*, look for a name made up of just the second syllable on. For example, for *Harel*, look for *Relle*.

11
The Sound of Double *L*

I have a friend who, thankfully, has a great sense of humor. She forgives friends, like me, for periodically reminding her of the day she told us she had several ancestors who were /fillies duh roy/. But it was really quite understandable. That's how the phrase *filles du roi looks* like it should be pronounced. So how *do* you pronounce the word *fille*?

There are many words in French with *ll* that actually make the /l/ sound, like *ville* for town and *tranquille* for calm. But there are also many words, especially those with an *i* before the *ll*, which change the *ll* to a /y/ sound, similar to Spanish. One of those words is *fille*, the French word for *daughter*, and *filles*, with an unpronounced *s* at the end for the plural, daughters. If you realized that with a silent *s*, both of those words sound exactly the same, you're right. (If you need a reminder about the silent consonant at the end of a word, see chapter 7.) If you're wondering how people know the difference between the singular and plural for the words *daughter* and *daughters* if they sound alike, you can tell by the article. *La fille* means 'the daughter,' singular; and les (pronounced /lay/) *filles* means 'the daughters,' plural. So "*the daughters of the king*" become *les filles du roi*.

$$\text{la fille} \quad = \quad \text{the daughter}$$

$$\text{les filles} \quad = \quad \text{the daughters}$$

Now let's apply this to surnames. A surname search for *Antailla*...(Figure 11-1)

Figure 11-1: Michael Antailla household, 1870 US population census, Springwell, Michigan; Series M593, Roll 710, page 391

...should also include *Antaya* (Figure 11-2).

Figure 11-2: Edouard Antaya household, 1870 US population census, Fall River, Massachusetts; series M593, Roll 604, page 300

A search for Aillot...(Figure 11-3)

Figure 11-3: Vivien and Juliet Aillot household, 1880 US population census, West Baton Rouge, Louisiana; Series T9, Roll 474, page 340

...should also include Ayotte (Figure 11-4).

Figure 11-4: Joseph Ayotte household, 1880 US population census, Lincoln, Rhode Island; series T9, Roll 1214, page 389

In both English and French, the letter *i* often substitutes for a *y*. So you'll see *Ayotte* spelled *Aiot*.

There are even instances of the *ll* being replaced with a *gu*. So *Mailly* can become *Maguy*.

Then there are the times when the *ll* is eliminated altogether. Brouillette becomes Bruette, or Guillette becomes Guiette.

There is one other thing to think about. If an Englishman heard someone pronounce the name Antailla as it looks, then he would probably spell the word with either a double or a single *l*.

Now let's compare Soundex codes:

Antailla	A534	Antaya	A530
Aillot	A430	Ayotte	A300

Keep this in mind when searching for lost ancestors. If you're looking for an ancestor with the /y/ sound in his name and can't find him, try looking for the *ll, l, y, i, gu,* or...nothing. And if you're looking for an ancestor with an *ll* in his name, try looking for that same name with a *y* in it. When doing Soundex searches, you need to complete two separate searches.

Tip for Use with Search Strategy Toolkit

When looking for surnames with the sound of /y/, the name could be spelled with an *ll, l, i, y, gu* or nothing.

12
The Sound of /Ā/

Many folks have ancestors with the surname Blais, roughly pronounced /Blay/ in French. Chapter 7 explained how a consonant at the end of a word does not sound unless it ends in a silent *e*. So the *s* at the end of *Blais* is silent. However, that means no matter which consonant appears at the end of the word, it is still pronounced the same way. The names Blait and Blaix are also pronounced /Blay/.

There are other letter combinations in French that also produce the equivalent of, or close approximation to, the /ā/ in English.

The name Haché ends with the /ā/ represented by the *é*. In French, the sounds may not be exactly the same as /ā/ in English, but when spoken by Americans, it tends to sound that way. Other French spellings that produce the /ā/ are names ending in *et* as in Beaudet, *er* as in Boucher, *ers* as in Angers, *ay* as in Betournay, and to some degree, *eil*. Although more authentically pronounced /ay-ee/, to an English speaker it more often shortens to /ā/, as in Beausoleil (Bo-so-lay').

-ais, -aies, -ait, -aix	as in Blais
-é	as in Haché
-et	as in Beaudet
-er	as in Boucher
-ers	as in Angers
-ay	as in Betournay
-eil, -eille	as in Beausoleil

I've known people here in the United States with the last name Blais, and it's always pronounced /Blaze/. To find that name in an index, such as the ProQuest HeritageQuest Online census indexes below, you would have to check the original spelling. But you'd also have to check all the different ways you'd make those sounds in English: Blays, Blaze, Blase, Blais or Blaize (Figure 12-1).

Surname	Given Name	Age	Sex	Race	Birthplace	State	County	Location	Year
BLAIS	ADELARD	49	M	W	CANA	CT	HARTFORD	9-WD HARTFORD	1930
BLAIS	ALBERT	40	M	W	CANA	CT	HARTFORD	9-WD HARTFORD	1930
BLAIS	ALPHEUS S	61	M	W	NY	CT	NEW LONDON	3-WD NEW LONDON	1930
BLAIS	ANNA	50	F	W	CANA	CT	WINDHAM	DANIELSON BORO	1930
BLAIS	ARTHUR	27	M	W	CANA	CT	NEW LONDON	GRISWOLD	1930

Surname	Given Name	Age	Sex	Race	Birthplace	State	County	Location	Year
BLAZE	NAPOLEON	24	M	W	CANA	MA	BERKSHIRE	ADAMS	1880

Figure 12-1: Spellings for /Blaze/

In English, there are a couple of ways to make the /ā/ at the end of a word. The most common is *ay* as in *today*. Then there's *ey* as in *they*. So what if the census enumerator asked someone his last name, and he heard /Blay/. If he himself were not French-Canadian, how would he write it? Blay? Bley? (Figure 12-2)

Surname	Given Name	Age	Sex	Race	Birthplace	State	County	Location	Year
BLAY	ALEXANDER	28		W	CANA	MA	SUFFOLK	BOSTON; 8-WD	1880
BLAY	CATHERINE	24		W	CANA	MI	WAYNE	DETROIT	1880
BLAY	CHARLES	25		W	CANA	MI	WAYNE	DETROIT	1880

Figure 12-2: Spelling for /Blay/

A check in the census index showed people whose last name is Boucher spelled *Bouchay*; people named Aubé spelled *Aubay*; and the name Beaupré spelled *Bopray*; letter for letter how it sounds (Figure 12-3).

Surname	Given Name	Age	Sex	Race	Birthplace	State	County	Location	Year
BOUCHAY	JOHN	70	M	W	CANA	MA	BRISTOL	1-WD FALL RIVER	1920

Surname	Given Name	Age	Sex	Race	Birthplace	State	County	Location	Year
AUBAY	OLDLAIDE	22		W	CANA	RI	PROVIDENCE	WOONSOCKET; 143-DIST	1880

Surname	Given Name	Age	Sex	Race	Birthplace	State	County	Location	Year
BOPRAY	ANGELINE	57		W	CANA	WI	WINNEBAGO	RUSHFORD	1880
BOPRAY	JOHN	44	M	W	CANA	NY	OSWEGO	GRANBY	1870
BOPRAY	JOSEPH	52	M	W	CANA	WI	MARINETTE	COLEMAN TWP	1900

Figure 12-3: Names spelled phonetically

Then there's the surname Duchesne/Duchene. Here you have an *e* or *es* followed by a consonant and a silent *e*. In French, the proper pronunciation is closer to /Doo-shĕn'/. But in America, /shĕn/ sounds more like /shāne/.

In some instances, you will find some rare spellings like *-ea*, *-eigh*, or *-y*. You might find the surname Gonyea, or you might see Bruleigh for Brulé or Cody for Coté.

So keep in mind all the different letter combinations that make the /ā/ in French as well as all the different ways to spell those sounds in English.

Tip for Use with Search Strategy Toolkit

Look for surnames with the French ways of spelling /ā/ *(-ais, -aies, -ait, -aix, -é, -et, -er, ers, -ay, eil,* or *-eille)* as well as the English combinations *(-ay, -a* + consonant + silent *e,* or *-ai* + consonant + silent *e, -ea, -ey, -e* + consonant + silent *-e, -es* + consonant + silent *-e, -eigh, -y).*

13
The Sound of /CH/

The *ch* letter combination in French does not make the same /ch/ sound as in English. It occasionally makes a /k/ sound, especially before the letter *r*, as in the surname Chretien. But most often it makes the /*sh*/ sound, as in the French words *chez* and *chien*. In surnames, this is true whether the *ch* is in the middle of a name like Beauchamp, or at the beginning like Chauvin. Failing to keep this in mind may prevent you from locating an ancestor in both print and digital indexes.

If you are looking for Chauvins, don't forget to try *Shauvin*, *Shovin*, and *Shoven*, among others, as you can see in these ProQuest HeritageQuest Online census indexes below (Figure 13-1). Although I never ran into this spelling in any of my family names, it is a possibility. So be aware.

Chenault can be found in the indexes as *Shano* (Figure 13-2).

If you've been searching for an Ambrose Chaubert, he's the only person in the 1860 US Population Census with his surname spelled *Shobare*.

In Chouinard, the *ou* after the *ch* adds a /w/ in the mix, causing Chouinard to show up as *Sweeney* in some records.

Surname	Given Name	Age	Sex	Race	Birthplace	State	County	Location	Year
SHAUVIN	ARTHUR	38	M	W	MA	MA	WORCESTER	WEBSTER	1920
SHAUVIN	DALPHIS	28	M	W	CANA	MT	DEER LODGE	4 & 5-TWP	1900
SHAUVIN	EMERY	49	M	W	CANA	MA	BRISTOL	1-WD FALL RVR	1910
SHAUVIN	MARTHA	73	F	W	CANA	MA	WORCESTER	WEBSTER	1920

Surname	Given Name	Age	Sex	Race	Birthplace	State	County	Location	Year
SHOVIN	AMIDY	11	M	W	NY	NY	CLINTON	PLATTSBURGH	1880
SHOVIN	AMIDY	46	M	W	CANA	NY	CLINTON	PLATTSBURGH	1880

Surname	Given Name	Age	Sex	Race	Birthplace	State	County	Location	Year
SHOVEN	ADLORE	40	M	W	IL	IL	KANKAKEE	1-WD KANKAKEE	1920
SHOVEN	ALFERD	3		W	WI	WI	VERNON	WEBSTER	1880
SHOVEN	ANDREW	52	M	W	CANA	IL	IROQUOIS	BEAVER TWP	1870
SHOVEN	ANDREW	61	M	W	CANA	IL	KANKAKEE	1-WD KANKAKEE	1910

Figure 13-1: Alternate spellings for the surname Chauvin

Surname	Given Name	Age	Sex	Race	Birthplace	State	County	Location	Year
SHANO	ALFONZIN	17		W	CANA	CT	WINDHAM	PUTNAM	1880
SHANO	ALICE	19	F	W	CO	CO	LAKE	1-WD LEADVILLE	1900
SHANO	ALUGEE	16		W	CANA	CT	WINDHAM	PUTNAM	1880

Figure 13-2: Alternate spelling for the surname Chenault

You must be just as vigilant for a *ch* located in the middle of a surname. Tachereau can be found in the census as *Tashro*. Others, like Michaud, evolved into the English name Mitchell where the *ch* became a *tch*.

In English, the /sh/ sound in some French names appears with a softer sound which approximates the /zh/ in English. This shows up as a *j* in names like Jabotte for Chabot. Some names like Chartier replace the *ch* with a *c* and become Carter in English.

So when you're looking for a name with a *ch* in it, first check for an *sh*. When you hear a name with /sh/, look for a *ch* as well. If that doesn't solve your problem, be sure to look for a *j-*, *c-*, *-tch*, or *sw-*.

Tip for Use with Search Strategy Toolkit

Check for an *sh* when your name has a *ch* in it, and vice versa. Also look for an alternate *j-*, *c-*, *-tch*, or *sw-*.

14
The Sound of an Initial /OU/

Even if you've never taken a French lesson in your life, I'm sure you are familiar with the French word for *yes*. Spelled *oui*, it's approximate pronunciation is /oo-ee/. English speakers tend to pronounce it as if it were spelled *wee*. *Oui, oui.* Wee-wee, yes, yes. The English ear has a difficult time distinguishing the subtle difference. Nevertheless, because English speakers *do* pronounce it with a /w/ sound, in English, the *w* and the *ou* become interchangeable.

There is a French surname Ouellette, pronounce /Wuh-let'/ in English. If a Ouellette in America told an English-speaking town clerk what his last name was, that clerk would have heard /Willette/, with an initial /w/ sound. So you need to also search for that surname beginning with a *w*. The end of the word could end with a *t*, a double *tt*, or a double *tt* followed by an *e*.

A similar surname, Ouimette, can be found in English records as *Wimette*. Be sure to also check for a double *m*, one or two *t*'s, and with or without the final *e*.

Working in reverse, if you have an ancestor in America with a last name such as Willette or Wimette, you must change your search in French records for a surname beginning with *Ou*. If you do not find what you're looking for using the *Ou*, search for Ouellette with an initial mute *h*, Houlette (see chapter 10).

If one of your ancestors was an English captive carried to Canada, you will often find him or her in the French records with a mutilated surname that looks nothing like the original in English. One of the captives named Weber appears in French records with the surname Ouabard, Ouabart, Houabart, and Houabard.

Waddens can be found as Ouadens. And the name William might be spelled Ouilem if it was not translated into the French word for William, which is Guillaume.

So if you've been having trouble finding given names or surnames beginning with the /w/ sound, be sure to check out that same name with an *ou* or an *hou*.

Tip for Use with Search Strategy Toolkit

When searching for a French name beginning with the letters *ou*, search in English records for *ou*, *w*, or *hou*.

15
The Sound of a Medial or Final /OU/

An *ou* in the middle of a French name makes the /oo/ sound heard in *mood*. But you'll run into some really creative spellings. Alternative English spellings would most likely be *u*, *oo*, or *ue*.

Boucher shows up in records as Boocher, Bucher, and Bushay. Latouche can be spelled Latoosh. Houle becomes Hool.

There are some rare misspellings where the *ou* is replaced with an *o* even though the two sounds are different. In English, you might find Bourdeau written as Bordo.

One comical misspelling is the French surname Poupard. Remember that the *d* is not pronounced because there is no *e* at the end. So if you have Poupard ancestors who migrated to America, the name shows up in the census exactly as it sounds, Poopar or Pooper.

When the *ou* comes in the middle of a multisyllable word, the *ou* can disappear altogether, as when Bourassa becomes Brasseau in

America. But since the vowels appear in the middle of the name, there shouldn't be a problem. Soundex search parameters are more concerned with consonant sounds.

However, sometimes when the *ou* appears in the final syllable, you will see several different combinations of consonants after it. If there is no *e* at the end, these consonants do not sound (see ch. 7). Take the surname *Ledoux*. The *x* is silent, so *Ledou* and *Ledoux* are pronounced the same. The letter combinations *oux*, *oulx*, *oult* and *oust* are at times pronounced the same, /oo/.

However, once consonants are added, Soundex searches *are* affected. When the enumerator heard the name Ledoux, he might have spelled it as he heard it, *Ladoo* or *Lado*. The Soundex code for that spelling is L300. If that same enumerator asked the family to spell the surname *Ledoux*, the Soundex code would change to L320.

There is another concern with surnames where one or more than one consonant follows the *ou* (as in Proulx, Prou, Proux, Prout, Proult, or Proust; Girou, Giroud, Giroult, Giroulx, Giroust, Giroux). For most of them, the last consonant or two are silent. However, it can change when the name ends in two consonants, like Proulx or Giroust. In some cases, the last consonant is silent, but the next to the last one sounds. So Proult would sound like /Prool/. You would pronounce Giroust as /Gĭ-roose'/. Note that the Soundex codes change for each different spelling. For example, Soundex codes (in order) for the various spellings of Proulx mentioned above are P642, P600, P620, P630, P634, and P623.

So remember to check out these alternative spellings for the /oo/ sound when hunting down those *ou* ancestors.

Tip for Use with Search Strategy Toolkit

Ou in the middle or at the end of a surname is pronounced /oo/. The sound may appear as *u, oo, ue,* or even *o*. When there are silent consonants at the end, the pronunciation is the same, but Soundex codes change. When a name ends in *ou* followed by two consonants, sometimes the next to the last one sounds while the last one is silent.

16
The Sound of /D/

My mother and her sevens siblings grew up speaking French in their household. But when my *mémère* died, that was the last I heard of conversational French within the family.

I read a post in the French-Canadian Descendants Facebook group[32]. The question was, "How much does the pronunciation of *maudit* vary? The way my dad said it was /mood-zee/." Apparently just hearing that word again brought back a lot of memories for several people. That post generated many comments, some hilarious, as people recalled their family's use of *maudit*.

Even though I did not know its exact meaning, as a kid I figured out that it was some sort of swear word. So I looked it up in an online French dictionary, and it gave the fairly tame definitions of *blasted* or *confounded*. I recall thinking it meant something a bit stronger than that. So when I visited my elderly aunt, I asked

---

[32] from August 22, 2014

her if she remembered the word and what it meant. She said she always figured it meant something like *damned*.

Quite a bit of the discussion centered around the pronunciation of the word, especially the sound of the letter *d*. It's the same as in my mother's rather rare maiden name, *Sourdif*.

My family spells the name *S-o-u-r-d-i-f*, but you will also see *Sourdiff*, *Sourdiffe*, and *Sourdive* (the way the original immigrant spelled it). Since my mother was the seventh of seven daughters followed by a boy, my uncle is one of the few in our vicinity still carrying that surname. After he married, his wife found it such a royal pain having to constantly spell the last name because no English speaker around here had a clue how to spell /Soods-eef/. As a result, she started pronouncing it /Sore-dĭf/. So for the last twenty years or so, I never heard /Soods-eef/ anymore; I heard /Sore-dĭf/.

A few years back, some friends and I took a research trip to Montréal. Since my great-grandfather Jules Sourdif came from the St-Jacques/St-Liguori region, I decided to drive there to see if I could find any distant cousins. Since the church was locked, I visited the St-Jacques fire station across the street. After all, firemen know just about everyone in town! They should know if any Sourdifs still lived there.

I walked over, and in my broken French asked if anyone knew of any /Sore-dĭfs/ in town. I got puzzled looks from every last one of them until it hit me. Even though that's the way I had heard the name pronounced for the last couple of decades, that's not how it would be pronounced in Quebec. So I grabbed my pedigree chart, pointed to Jules, and repeated the word /Soods-eef/. They all started nodding their heads, saying, "Oui, oui, Sourdif, Sourdif." Apparently someone with that surname worked at the town hall. A fireman was nice enough to show me the way there, just to find that it was closed for the afternoon.

But then I drove on to St. Liguori and actually met a couple of distant cousins there. So it was definitely worth the drive and the effort to communicate.

Now let's talk about this letter *d*. In the word *maudit* /mood-zee/ and the surname *Sourdif*, it sounds more like a /dz/ than just the

/d/. Is it something that could cause a roadblock for us as we research our French-Canadian families?

First, in Parisian French, the differences between the French /d/ and the English /d/ are not as pronounced. But in Canadian French, before the /ee/ sound, the letter *d* makes a /dz/ sound. If the nasally /ain/ or /in/ sound follows the *d* (see chapter 17), then the /d/ sound more closely resembles the English /d/.

Confused? Let me give you some examples. The surnames Godin and Baudin both make a /d/ sound like that in English. The *d* is followed by the nasally /in/. But surnames like *Sourdif, Sedilot, Paradis*, and *Cadieux* all make the /dz/ sound, and all are followed by the letter *i* which makes the /ee/ sound (Figure 16-1).

Surname with -din; sounds like English /d/	Surnames with -di-; sounds like /dz/
Godin	Sourdif
Beaudin	Sedilot
Desjardins	Paradis
Cardin	Cadieux
	Also: Acadien (evolved into Cajun)

Figure 16-1: Surnames with the letter d

Another example is the word *Acadien*. It's pronunciation /a-ca-dzien/ evolved in the southern United States into *Cajun*.

Could this pronunciation cause us difficulty in finding ancestors in an American census index? Let's take a look at the name *Paradis*. As we learned in chapter 7, the final *s* is not pronounced because there is no silent *e* after it. Therefore it is pronounced /pa-ra-dzee/. In central Massachusetts there are descendants from this line who Anglicized the word by adding an *e* to the end and pronouncing it /pa-ra-dīce/. But remember, when they first came down from Québec, they would have pronounced it /pa-ra-dzee/.

In the 1910 census we find a 17-year-old young man by the name of Frederick Parazee. In 1900 there is a William Parazee.

In the 1910 census, Frederick's entry clearly states he and his parents are from French Canada. Could this Frederick Parazee in America be Frederick Paradis in Québec?

Something to keep in mind if you are hunting for lost ancestors with a *di* in their surname.

Tip for Use with Search Strategy Toolkit

If an ancestor's surname has a *di* in it, be prepared to search for a *z* instead.

17
The Sound of
/AIN/ and /IN/

In English we pronounce *ain* as /āne/ and *in* as / ĭn/. In French, these two letter combinations make approximately the same sound, but with a nasally twist to it. It's a sound that is foreign to English speakers. For the sound of /ain/, try saying *ain*, but stop before the *n* sound. For /in/, say *in*, but leave off the *n*.

Try typing the surname Beaudin into a text-to-speech utility, such as one mentioned in chapter 3. Make sure you've chosen the Canadian French speaker, and listen to it a couple of times.

A *d* in front of this nasally syllable makes a /d/ sound similar to that in English as opposed to the /dz/ sound you hear in front of the /ee/ sound (see chapter 16).

Now when you're searching for ancestors, it can get a bit tricky. You will see the /ain/ sound spelled either *ain* or *in*. They're very interchangeable in surnames. For example, the name *Alain* can also appear as *Alin*. But, it's not that simple, because there are also many other letter combinations used in place of the letters *ain* or *in*. The same surname *Alain* can also end with an *en* in English.

One Maple Stars and Stripes podcast listener, Steve Moray, wrote in with this story:

> I had a brick wall with my Canadian immigrant ancestor Israel Morey (you'll notice the "Morey" has evolved to "Moray" in the intervening generations), and had never been able to figure out where he was from in Canada, or what his parents' names were. A few years ago I had my dad do a Y-DNA test to see if it might be able to shed any more light on the subject. There are quite a few English Moreys in Canada whom I thought were the best candidates to be relatives, so much to my surprise all my dad's matches came back with the last name *Morin*.

So now we have to add *ay* and *ey* as possible endings for surnames ending in either of these nasally sounds. Names might convert from Aubin to Obey, Beaudoin to Bodway, Malouin to Maulway. Then there's the surname Jodoin which we find spelled both Jodway and Jodware.

Because the final *n* is not sounded in these names, the words end with a 'hanging' vowel sound. This has caused English speakers to sometimes spell these names with the *a* or *ah* ending as in Babba for Babin and Boutah for Boutin. The name may also take on the letters *aw* such that Gamelin becomes Gumlaw.

What about names with the *ain* or *in* located in the beginning or middle of the word? The *gain* in Bourgainville sometimes appears as *guin*. The *u* added to the middle syllable keeps the hard /g/ sound (see chapter 21). The *ain* in *Chainié* can also be *en*, *egn*, or *esn*. The *Saint* in Saintmarc can even change to *Cinq*.

When a word ends in *ain* and you add an *e* to the end, you now pronounce the *n* sound. It softens the nasal sound. So *ain* now sounds more like /ĕn/. Therefore, *Chapdelaine* can also end in *-leine* or *-lene*. The same with *Dechene*, which can end with *-aine*, *-ene*, *-enes*, *-enne*, *-esne*, *-aines*, *-ennes*, or *-esnes*.

Tip for Use with Search Strategy Toolkit

The sounds formed by the letters *ain* and *in* in French have no equivalent in the English language. At the end of a name, look for *ain, in, en, ey, ay, are, a, ah,* or *aw.* In the middle of a word, search also for *uin, en, egn,* or *esn.* When followed by an *e,* this sound can be spelled *aine, ene, enes, enne, esne, aines, ennes,* or *esnes* without the nasal quality.

18
The Sound of /QUE/

Native French speakers will pronounce the French-Canadian province in Canada as /kĕ-bĕc/. English speakers pronounce it with an initial /kw/ sound, /kwĕ-bĕc/. Think back to when you were in grammar school and you were first exposed to the word *antique*. If you were like me, you just couldn't imagine how the letters *que* produced the /k/ sound instead of /kyoo/.

Keep this in mind when you transition from American records back to Québec records. If your surname has a /k/ sound in English, think of substituting those letters with a *que* in French.

Now in the opposite direction, if your French surname ends with a *que*, think of the different letter combinations in English that make a /k/ sound. In English records, look for a *qu, c, k*, and *ck*. Any of these could be a substitution for the *qu* in a French surname.

Could the French name *Beique* show up in English records as *Beck*?

Or *Levesque* as *Laveck*?

Could the *Buskey* found in American censuses really be the French name *Bousquet*?

And *Larock* is most likely *Laroque* in French.

When the qu- comes at the beginning of a name, search English records for a *c* (Canell for Quesnel) or a *k* (Kinville for Quenneville).

When located in the middle of a name, expect to find a *c* as in Pelican for Péloquin.

Now lets combine that with the nasally sound we learned about in chapter 17. A final *-ain* or *-in* makes a unique nasal sound that might be described as the sound of /a/ in *an* without pronouncing the /n/. So take the surname Quintin. How do you think that would be pronounced in French? Try pronouncing /can-tan/, leaving off the /n/ at the end of each syllable. How would you most likely spell that in English?

In American census records, there are several people with birthplaces in Canada whose last name is spelled Cantin or Cantan. Could those be some missing Quintins?

Remember to type a French name into a text to speech utility, listen carefully to the sounds it makes, and translate those into English letters. And don't stop at just one variation. Try every spelling variation for letter sounds that you can come up with, and it will increase your chances of success.

Tip for Use with Search Strategy Toolkit

When searching for French surnames with the /k/ sound in English, search for records with a *que* instead. In English records, look for *qu*, *c*, *k*, or *ck*.

19
The Sound of /ER/ and /ERT/

Let's review what we learned in chapter 7. In general, a final consonant in French is not sounded unless:

- ❖ that final consonant is a *c*, *r*, *f*, or *l* (remember the consonants in the word *CaReFuL*), or,

- ❖ the final consonant is followed by a silent *e*.

In that chapter, I used the surname Collet, pronounced /co-lay'/, as an example. The name picked up an *e* when my ancestors migrated to America and became Collette, pronounced /co-lĕt'/.

With that in mind, let's take a look at the name Robert, pronounced /rob'-ert/ in English, but /ro-bair'/ in French. The *t* is not sounded because there is no *e* after it. An *ert* makes the sound /air/. That is what an English-speaking town clerk or a census enumerator would hear.

In the 1880 US census population schedules, you'll find a Joseph Robair in Michigan (Figure 19-1), an Adeline Robear from

Vermont (Figure 19-2), a Dolphus Robare in New York (Figure 19-3), and an Albert Robert (Figure 19-4; pronounced /ahl-bair ro-bair/; his parents apparently had a sense of humor). All of these surnames are spelled differently.

Surname	Given Name	Age	Sex	Race	Birthplace	State	County	Location	Year
ROBAIR	JOSEPH	24		W	CANA	MI	MARQUETTE	2-WD. ISHPEMING	1880

Figure 19-1: Joseph Robair (images from HeritageQuest Online)

Surname	Given Name	Age	Sex	Race	Birthplace	State	County	Location	Year
ROBEAR	ADELINE	48		W	CANA	VT	CHITTENDEN	BURLINGTON, 88-DIST	1880

Figure 19-2: Adeline Robear (images from HeritageQuest Online)

Figure 19-3: Dolphus Robare (images from HeritageQuest Online)

Surname	Given Name	Age	Sex	Race	Birthplace	State	County	Location	Year
ROBERT	ALBERT	10		W	CANA	NH	HILLSBOROUGH	MANCHESTER	1880

Figure 19-4: Albert Robert: (images from HeritageQuest Online)

If you are searching for the surname Robert in an online database that uses a Soundex based search function, the Soundex code for *Robert* is R163. However the Soundex code for the other three name variations is R160. (If you need to remind yourself how Soundex codes work, refer back to chapter 4.)

There are quite a few French surnames that end with the letters *e-r-t*. They also appear in English records spelled a variety of ways. The English surname Hebert (Hee'-bert) is pronounced /abair'/ in French and shows up in some census records spelled *Abair*. The surname pronounced /o-bair'/, usually spelled in French as Hobert (see chapter 10 for the lesson on the mute H) or Aubert, is spelled *Obair* in some records. In similar ways, Boisvert is spelled *Boisvair*; Joubert is *Joubear*, and Gilbert is *Gilbair* or *Gilbare*.

Be sure to keep this in mind as you search in English records for a French ancestor with a surname ending in the sound /air/.

Tip for Use with Search Strategy Toolkit

When English speakers write what they hear, a name like Auger could end in *er* or *ert*; but you might also find the endings *air*, *aire*, *ar*, *are*, or *ear*. Though less frequent, you might also see the *er* and *ert* replaced with an *e*, *ea*, *ee*, *ia*, *a*, *ie*, *y*, *ey*, or *ay*. Baulier might appear as *Baulia*; Bélanger as *Belongy*; Boucher as *Bouchey* or *Bouchay*; Durocher as *Durochie*.

In reverse, if you have an American surname ending in *air*, *are*, *aire*, *ar*, or other abovementioned letter combinations, check for French surnames that end in -*er* or -*ert*.

20
The Sound of /EU/, /IEU/, and /IEUX/

In chapter 8, I told the story about my search for my maternal grandmother's Mathieu family. The problem occurred because of the way English speaking people heard the French-spoken /th/ sound. But a secondary problem occurred with the sound made by the *ieu* at the end of the word.

Think of the sound that an *e* makes in an English word that ends in *er*. Pronounce the *e* without adding the /r/ sound at the end and it's pretty close to the /eu/ sound in French, as in Port-n*eu*f.

You'd pronounce *ieu* as /ee-eu/. But that sound is foreign to English speakers. They tend to replace it with the sound /i-er/, adding the /r/ to the end.

So when you are searching for French names that end in /eu/ or /ieu/, remember that in English, you might find the name with an *er* or *ier* ending. That also changes its Soundex code. In

American census records, Beaulieu, with a Soundex code of B400, appears as *Bolier*, now with the Soundex code of B460.

In French, some surnames that end in *ieu* have an *x* at the end. Since there is no *e* after it, the *x* is silent; so the pronunciation is the same. We have the French surnames Levieux, Lesieux, and Lemieux, all ending in *-ieux*, found in the census ending in *ier*, or in some cases, *yer*.

You will sometimes see an *f* after the *eu*, as in *Leboeuf*. For this name, pronounce the second syllable as /berf/, eliminating the /r/ sound.

Perhaps because of the similarity in spelling, some names ending in *eu* are written in America as *eau*. The letters *eau* have a completely different sound in French, that of a long /ō/. So you will occasionally see *eau*, *eaux*, and *o* in place of *eu*.

Other possible spellings are *ey*, *ie*, and *y*. Belhumeur is sometimes spelled *Belhumere* or *Belhumore*. Beaulieu appears as *Beaulia* or *Beaulio*. In my case, my maternal grandmother's surname Mathieu shows up occasionally as *ue*, *ew*, and *ews*.

So keep all those endings in mind as you search for your ancestors whose surnames end in the complicated letter combinations of *eu*, *ieu* or *ieux*.

Tip for Use with Search Strategy Toolkit

Surnames ending in *-eu*, *-ieu*, or *-ieux* may show up in American records with a variety of letter combinations: *er*, *ier*, *yer*, *eau*, *eaux*, *o*, *ey*, *ie*, *y*, *ere*, *ore*, *a*, *ue*, *ew*, or *ews*.

21
The Sound of /G/

If you have an ancestral surname with a *g* in it, the sound it makes depends on the following letter.

In English, we say that the *g* makes either a hard or a soft *g* sound. The hard *g* is the sound you hear in *gather*. The soft *g* is the sound in *gymnasium* (Figure 21-1).

In French, the soft *g* makes an even softer sound than in English, indicated in linguistics by /zh/. Think of the sound you hear in the middle of *measure*. The sound /zh/ that you hear is like the soft *g* sound in French.

Whenever a *g* is followed by another consonant like *r* or *l*, it makes the hard *g* sound as in the surnames *Grandmont* and *Gladu*. However, in the surname Gladu, the name has also appeared in English records as *Clodgo* with a *cl* replacing the *gl* (Figure 21-2).

You also hear a hard *g* sound in front of an *a*, *o*, or *u*, as in *Gallant*, *Godin*, and *Guibord*. Note that in *Guibord*, the *u* helps to retain the hard /g/ sound. Otherwise the name *Gibord* would be pronounced /zhee-bor/. You can sometimes also replace the *gu* with a *y* (Guertin to Yartin) or a *d* (Guyon to Dion).

/g/in English		Example
Hard g	/g/	gather
Soft g	/j/	gymnasium

/g/ in French		Example
Hard g	/g/	Gauthier
Soft g	/zh/	Gervais

/gn/ in French		Example
gn	/ny/	Carignan

Figure 21-1: The sounds of g

In front of an *e*, *i*, or *y*, you will hear the softer /zh/ sound. So Gervais is pronounced /zher-vay'/. Gingras is /zhin-grah/; Baugy is /bō-zhee'/. English speakers usually write the /zh/ as a *j*, especially in the initial position.

Keep in mind when using Soundex, the code begins with the first letter of the surname. Since the soft /g/ sound in French sounds most like the English /j/, the enumerator may have spelled Jervais and Jingras instead of Gervais and Gingras.

Gervais should have the Soundex code of G612. But if the enumerator wrote it with a *j* as the initial letter, the Soundex code becomes J612. Gingras becomes J526 instead of G526.

There is one other tricky thing about the letter *g*. In front of an *n*, it makes the same sound as in its fellow Romance languages of Spanish and Italian. Most people are familiar with the *tilde* over the *n* in Spanish. It's the little squiggly mark found above the *n* in the word *señor*. The name of the letter *n* in Spanish is *en-ne*, but the *n* with the *tilde* on top is called *en-ye*. Right there you have the difference in sound. An *enye* sounds like the *ny* in our word *canyon*. So a *g* in front of an *n* makes this same /n-y/ sound in Spanish, Italian, and French.

Sounds of French /g/		
Before	**Sound**	**Example**
R	hard	Grandmont
L	hard	Gladu
A	hard	Gallant
O	hard	Godin
U	hard	Guibord
E	soft	Gervais
I	soft	Gingras
Y	soft	Baugy
N	/ny/	Carignan

Figure 21-2: Sounds of French /g/

An example is the regiment that came over in the 17th century to control the Iroquois, the Carignan /car-een-yahn/-Salière Regiment. The surname Agnier is pronounced /ahn-yay'/. In the surname Agnier, you do not hear a /g/ sound at all, yet the Soundex system would record a numeral for that letter, as well as for the *n* and *r*. If you type the name into a Soundex converter the way it sounds, and the way an enumerator may have heard it, it receives a Soundex code of A500. But if you type it in the way it is spelled, the code is A256. Something to keep in mind when using Soundex-based search engines.

In a medial position, as in the surname Auger, the *g* takes the sound of /zh/. We've already seen that a *j* often replaces the /zh/ sound in English words. However, in surnames like Auger and Bergeron, an *sh* sometimes represents the sound of the *g* (Oshia and Bashaw).

121

Tip for Use with Search Strategy Toolkit

The letter *g* makes different sounds. The spelling changes based on the sound.

Hard *g*: *g*, *cl* for *gl*, *gu*, *y*, *d*

Soft *g*: *g*, *j*

/n-y/: *gn*

Medial *g*: *g*, *j*, *sh*

22
The Sound of /EUIL/ and /EUILLE/

There are letter combinations in French that have Anglophones shaking their heads. Examples are the letters *euil* and *euille*. How many of you have run into words with those letter combinations and didn't have a clue how to get your tongue around them?

Pronounced /oo-ee/ (/oo/ as in *good*, not *mood*), it is not a sound that comes naturally to English speakers. Americans tended to substitute the closest English sound of /oy/.

In chapter 11, we learned that a double-*l* most closely resembles the English /y/. Surnames with the letters *euil* or *euille* in them, like d'Argenteuil, Vertefeuille, or Bellefeuille, caused many problems for English-speaking town clerks and census enumerators. Writing what they heard, a sound similar to /oy/, resulted in the letters *oy* replacing the *euil*.

We see this in the 1900 US census in Tacoma, Washington. Four of the five members of the Bellfoy family are born in French-Canada. Can you guess what that name would be in Canada? I would definitely search for *Bellefeuille* in Canadian records (Figure 22-1).

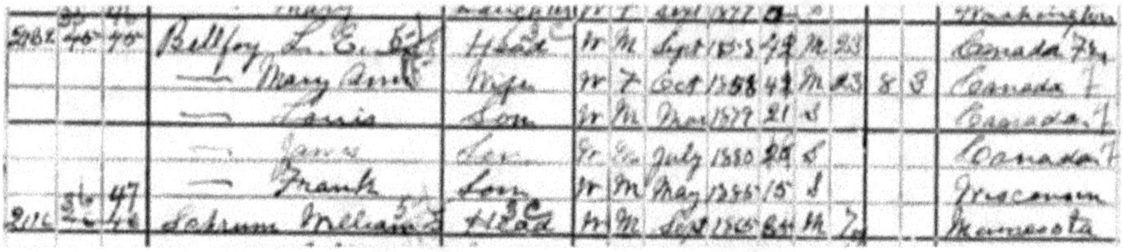

Figure 22-1: The Bellfoy (Bellefeuille) family in the 1900 US population census schedule for Tacoma, WA, from HeritageQuestOnline

So if you have a French family in Canada with a surname with the letters *-euil* or *-euille*, look for an *-oy* in American records. Conversely, if your Franco-American family's surname ends in *-oy*, search for *euil* or *euille* in Canadian records.

Tip for Use with Search Strategy Toolkit

When a Franco-American surname ends in /oy/, search in French records for the letters *euil* or *euille*. If a French name includes the letters *euil* or *euille*, look for the name spelled with an *oy* in English records.

23
The C-Cedille (ç)

A little tail can make a big difference!

The French language, like English, includes the letter *c*. But French has an extra letter that looks very much like a *c*, but with a little tail that hangs down from the bottom of the letter: Ç, ç. We call this a *c-cédille*, or *cédille*.

Let's back up a bit and look at English pronunciation. In English we have what's called the hard *c* and the soft *c* sound. The hard *c* sounds like the letter /k/ and is found usually in words where it precedes the letters *a*, *o*, and *u* as in *cat*, *cot*, and *cut*.

The soft *c* sounds like the letter /s/ and comes before the letters *e*, *i*, and *y* as in *independence*, *Pacific*, and *cycle*.

In English, there are exceptions to every rule, and sometimes even exceptions to the exceptions, but those rules apply most of the time.

In French there are similar rules. When a *c* appears before an *a*, *o*, or *u*, it makes a /k/ sound as in *Acadie*, *colonie*, and *cultivateur*. In front of an *e, i,* or *y,* you hear the sound of /s/. Think of *France, merci,* and *Montmorency*.

That is, usually. But not always.

There are some words where the *c* comes before an *a, o,* or *u,* and the speaker pronounces an /s/ sound instead of the /k/ sound. In writing, we show this by using a *cédille*.

Think of the word *Français* where the *c* is before an *a.* What sound do you hear? *Français.* Or the name *François.* Or *deçu.* In each of those words the *c* makes an /s/ sound, not the expected /k/ sound. To force this difference in sound, the French language uses a *c-cédille* instead of a plain ol' *c.* This is your reminder to go against the norm and pronounce the word with an /s/ sound.

The surname spelled *Marçolet* is not pronounced /mark-o-lay/, but rather /mar-so-lay/.

When you are searching for ancestors in an online index and your surname has a *c-cédille* in it, search also for an *s* instead of a *k*.

The French C		
Placement of Letter *C*	Sound	Examples
c in front of *e, i, y*	/s/	France, merci, Montmorency
c in front of *a, o, u*	/k/	Acadie, colonie, cultivateur
Ç or *ç* in front of *a, o, u*	/s/	Français, François, deçu

Figure 23-1: The French C

Tip for Use with Search Strategy Toolkit

If a French surname has a *c* before an *e, i,* or *y,* look for an *s* in English records. If the *c* comes before an *a, o,* or *u,* look for a *k.* If a *c-cédille* (Ç, ç) comes before an *a, o,* or *u,* look for an *s.*

24
The Sound of /OI/

I admit that one of the hardest words for me to pronounce in French is the word *roi*. You do not say /roy/. If that were true, it would be so easy. But, no.

First, /r/ is not the same as in English. Instead of pursing the lips, the mouth is more relaxed, and the sound comes from the back of the throat. Then, the *oi* is pronounced as /wah/ (not exact, but close). Think of the pronunciation of the Loire River in France. Pronouncing /r/ followed by /wah/ is very difficult for most English speakers.

So it's no wonder that *oi* surnames have alternative spellings.

The sound it makes can also vary because of the letter that follows it. We've already discussed in chapter 17 how an *n* after an *oi* produces a nasally sound, as in Beaudoin. This is totally different from the sound it usually makes.

At the end of a word, the *oi* appears in English as *oy*. It can be spelled *oy* in French as well. Examples are the surnames Roi/Roy and Defoi/Defoy. The *oi/oy* is interchangeable in a medial position as well, as in Cournoier/Cournoyer. Because the *y* is not counted in Soundex codes (see chapter 4), the code remains the same no matter the spelling.

We discussed in chapter 7 that a final consonant does not sound without a silent *e* after it. You will often see the *oi* followed by an *s* or a *t*. *Boi* and *Bois* sound the same, so Boileau and Boisleau are the same surname. Because of the *s*, however, each surname would have a different Soundex code. Boileau is B400, and Boisleau is B240.

Many of our ancestors with English roots went by the surname or *dit* name Langlois. This also appears as Langlais.

Here in America, there is another common variation. If your ancestor has the surname Benway, look for him in French records as Benoit.

Tip for Use with Search Strategy Toolkit

The sound produced by the letters *oi* are written in records as *oi*, *oy*, *ois*, *oit*, *ais*, and *way*.

Part 3
Understanding Language
Peculiarities

25
Dit Names

Dit.

It may be a small word, but for native English speakers, it's an often mispronounced French word. Most Americans say it as if it rhymes with /sĭt/ and call it /dĭt/. But I'd like to refer you back to chapter 7. Here you learned that final consonants not followed by an *e* are silent. So rather than pronouncing it /dĭt/, you should pronounce it closer to /dzē/. (The d makes a /dz/ sound because it's followed by the /ē/. See chapter 16 for more information.)

Romance vs Germanic

Now we can add another level to this. French is a Romance language. That does not mean that it's the language of lovers. It means it comes from the language of the ancient Romans, which, of course, was Latin. French, Spanish, Portuguese, Italian, and Romanian, are all Romance languages. That means that those languages share a similar structure.

English, on the other hand, is a Germanic language. If you recall your European history, the Romans pulled out of Britain in the early 5th-century AD. The following decades saw incursions by the Angles and Saxons from what is today the area in and around Germany. They invaded, settled there, and left their language behind.

Since the English language comes from German, it is structured differently than French. An example of this has to do with adjectives. In English we put our adjectives before the nouns that they describe, for example, "the white dog." But in Romance languages, the adjectives come after the nouns. This means we would literally translate it as "the dog white."

Masculine vs Feminine

Another major difference in the structure of the languages is that Romance languages categorize their nouns as masculine or feminine. This does not necessarily correspond with the gender of the item. Not all objects *have* a gender. The French word for "hat" is *chapeau*. It's a masculine noun, even though in English we don't perceive a hat as having a gender. The word *maison*, which means "house," is feminine, although we don't tend to think of a house as having a gender either. And in French, the house itself doesn't, but the word does.

Any adjectives describing those nouns have to be in the corresponding masculine or feminine form. For example, the article *le* is the masculine form of "the"; the article *la* is the feminine form of "the." In English, we use "the" in front of any noun or adjective: the ball; the big, brown dog. It doesn't matter.

But in French, we would use the masculine article *le* in front of the masculine noun *chapeau, le chapeau.* In front of the feminine noun *maison*, we would use the feminine *la, la maison. Blanc* is the masculine form of the word "white"; *blanche* is the feminine form of the adjective "white." So it would be *le chapeau blanc*, all masculine forms of the words for "the white hat"; but *la maison blanche*, all feminine forms of the words, for "the white house." Often, but not always, the difference between the masculine form of an adjective and the feminine form is the addition of an *e* at the end.

So why do we have to know about masculine and feminine nouns and adjectives in order to understand about *dit* names? Well, *dit* is the masculine form and is used in reference to men. *Dite* is the feminine form and is used to refer to females. The feminine form is pronounced /dzēt/ because of the e at the end. *Dit* is pronounce /dzē/ unless the following word begins with a vowel sound. Then you pronounce it the same way as the feminine form.

Women could also use *dite* names. Antoine Latour dit Forget's daughter, Denise, used Latour *dite* Forget in the majority of records in which she appears.

Some people also had *dit/dite* names for their given names, as in Marguerite dite Julie Bousquet.

26
L + Apostrophe

In the French language, there is something called *élision*. The closest thing to it in English would be a contraction. It occurs when you drop a vowel if the next word begins with either a vowel or the mute *h*. (See chapter 10 for a review of the mute *h*.) So in English, it would be as if, instead of saying /the elephant/, we said, /thelephant/, as if it were one word.

So the French words for "the friend," *le ami*, become *l'ami*. The *e* in *le* is removed. *Le oncle*, "the uncle" in English, becomes *l'oncle* (Figure 26-1).

This is very important to understand when searching for your family in indexes. Surnames can be written with or without the *l* and with or without the apostrophe. It can be written one way in the record and another way in the index. You must check all possible spellings.

Sometimes the surname keeps the article; sometimes it doesn't. A man by the name of George L'Anglais lived in Burlington, Vermont, in 1920. His last name was written in the census with

In French...	...should be...	...but becomes
the friend	le ami	l'ami
the uncle	le oncle	l'oncle

Figure 26-1: French élisions

an L-apostrophe-capital A. If you search the index in HeritageQuest Online for the name George L'Anglais spelled that way, you will draw a blank even though that's how his name is spelled in the census. You *will* find him in the index, however, as George Langlais, without the apostrophe. If you search for him correctly with the apostrophe in his name you will not find him. If you search for him incorrectly without the apostrophe, you will be successful. That's why genealogists have to think creatively!

In the 1870 census for Rich Bar Township, California, there is a Frenchman by the name of Peter Anglais, no *L*, no apostrophe.

In 1910 in Minneapolis City, Minnesota, lived Rosalie L'Evesque, with an *L* and an apostrophe. Yet in the index, she appears as Rosalie Evesque, no *L*, no apostrophe.

The surname L'évesque in Québec was spelled with or without the apostrophe. A search in the HeritageQuest Online census index for the surname L'évesque with the apostrophe brought up six results from the 1940 census. A search for the name Lévesque without the apostrophe brought up over 6000 results. A search for Levesque without the *L* or the apostrophe, in other words, beginning with the letter *E*, produced nine results. So you can see how a search for Lévesque without the apostrophe, the more common way the name is spelled, would eliminate fifteen other possibilities for your missing ancestor.

This next item does not pertain just to French-Canadian genealogy. It is something you should keep in mind whenever you are searching an index for a given name or a surname beginning with an *L*.

Several years ago a friend of mine was looking for her grandfather in the 1910 census. She knew he was there; she knew she should be able to find him. But he did not show up in the index. When she told me his first name was Luke, I suggested she go back into the index, run the same search again, and this time look for a grandfather with the first name of Suke. There he was. In the handwriting of a century ago, the handwritten capital *L* and *S* were very similar. So in our Lévesque case, a search for Sevesque, beginning with an *S* instead of an *L*, resulted in 15 possibilities.

So if you have ancestors with that *L'* at the beginning of their names, be sure to search for the surname both with and without the apostrophe, with and without the *L*, and if you still can't find them, try the name with an initial *S* instead.

27

Surnames
with De, Des, and D'

In chapter 25, you learned that the French word for "the" differs depending on whether the noun it's describing is masculine or feminine. You saw that we use the article *la* before a feminine noun and *le* before a masculine noun. In chapter 11, we learned that when the noun is plural, "the" becomes *les* (Figure 27-1).

Words for "the" (depends on gender and number of the noun it describes)			
Feminine	*la*	*la maison*	the house
Masculine	*le*	*le chien*	the dog
Plural	*les*	*les chiens*	the dogs

Figure 27-1: French articles

The preposition *de* means "of" or "from" and indicates possession. In front of a feminine noun, you would say *de la fille* for "of the daughter." In front of a masculine noun, the *de le* becomes *du*, as in *du chien* instead of *de le chien*. We see it also in *Archives*

National du Québec. (See chapter 30 for further information.) In front of a plural noun, *de les* becomes *des*. "Of the dogs" is written as *des chiens* (Figure 27-2).

Words for "of" or "from" (depends on gender and number of the noun it describes)			
Feminine	*de la*	*de la maison*	of the house
Masculine	*du* (not *de le*)	*du chien*	of the dog
Plural	*des* (not *de les*)	*des chiens*	of the dogs

Figure 27-2: French prepositions with articles

How does this apply to genealogy?

Some surnames or *dit* names indicate a person's origins. It might indicate where he resided or where he was born. An example is Decelle, meaning "from Celle," or Denoyon meaning "from Noyon." We also see Desnoyers for "from Les Noyers" and Dubourg for "from Le Bourg."

So how do we apply this when searching in indexes for missing ancestors? When searching for ancestors whose surnames begin with *De*, *Des*, or *D'*, keep the following in mind:

❖ The *De* may or may not be present in the original record and/or the index.

   Delahaye/Lahaye

   Demontigny/Montigny

❖ The *Des* may include the *s* in some records but not in others.

   Desjadon/Dejadon

   Desloge/Deloge

❖ The Des may be omitted all together.

   Desmarais/Marais

A *de* in front of a vowel becomes *d'*. You will often find surnames in French beginning with *d'* written in English records without the apostrophe. D'Aragon became Daragon and then Dragon. D'Auberville became Dauberville.

> D'Aragon/Daragon/Dragon
>
> d'Auberville/Dauberville

Soundex

In surnames like Desjadon/Dejadon and Desloge/Deloge, the presence or absence of that *s* will affect that surname's Soundex code. Desloge with the *s* is D242. Deloge without the *s* is D420. It makes a big difference when searching online databases. If you need a reminder about Soundex codes, see chapter 4.

28
Gender Clues

In chapter 7 we discussed how adding an *e* to the end of the word *dit* to form *dite* changed the pronunciation of the word. It also changed the gender from masculine to feminine. The word *vert*, French for "green," modifies a masculine noun, but *verte* describes a feminine noun. When we add an *e* to the end of a noun or adjective, it often changes the gender of that word from masculine to feminine. The presence or absence of that final *e* can also provide clues in documents.

How can we use that knowledge of gender clues to help us when trying to read parish registers? Why is it even more important to search for the original records instead of relying on repertoires?

Some French-Canadian given names have a direct correlation to English names. Examples are Edouard and Edward, Olivier and Oliver. But some French-Canadian given names are totally unfamiliar to English speakers, names like Onésime, Trefflé, and Ozine. Many times I researched in repertoires and came across a new child for a couple. When I entered that child into my genealogy software program, I had no idea whether to list that child as male or female because I was unfamiliar with the name. In most published repertoires, you don't have access to the clues that you have in the original parish records.

Clues in Baptism Records

An original baptism record usually begins with the date. Then the priest writes in French, "by we" (*par nous*), "the undersigned priest" (*prêtre soussigné*), "was baptized" (*a eté baptisé*) [the name of the child] "born" (*né* or *née*) [today, yesterday, or whenever]. The French words for "was baptized" are *a eté baptisé*. If *baptisé* ends in an *e accent aigu* (é), then the baptized child is a male. If *baptisée* ends in an *e accent aigu* followed by another *e* (*ée*), then the child is female (Figure 28-1).

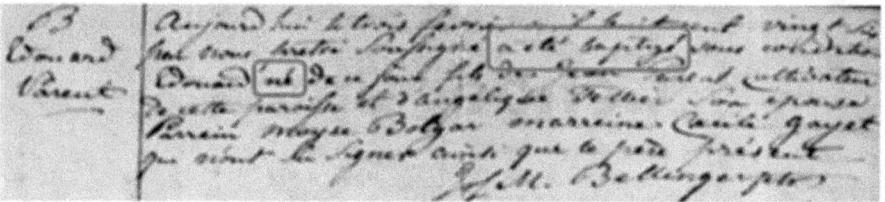

Figure 28-1: Gender clues in baptism records; the words *baptizé* and *né* indicate that this child is a male

Look for the word *par* before *nous*. If there is no *par*, and all you see is *nous prêtre soussigné avons baptisé*, then the above does not apply. The word *baptisé* is not modifying the child who was baptised. Instead it is part of a verb phrase, "...we, the undersigned priest, have baptised..."

The next clue in the same record is the word for "born." *Né* means the child is a boy, and *née* means the baby is a girl.

See Figure 28-2 for gender clues in baptism records.

Clues in Marriage Records

There are clues in marriage records also. When the records are hard to read, scan until you find the word *fils*. You are now looking at the groom's information. The word *fille* indicates the

Gender clues in baptism records	
a été baptisé	"was baptised," referring to a boy child
a été baptisée	"was baptised," referring to a girl child
ondoyé	a boy child was conditionally baptized
ondoyée	a girl child was conditionally baptized
jumeaux	twins, either both boys or a boy and a girl
jumelles	twin girls
né	born (boy)
née	born (girl)

Figure 28-2: Gender clues in baptism records

bride's section of the record. If the groom is legally of age, he was referred to as a *fils majeur*. An adult bride was referred to as a *fille majeure*. A groom who is not of age was a *fils mineur*, but the bride was a *fille mineure* (Figure 28-3).

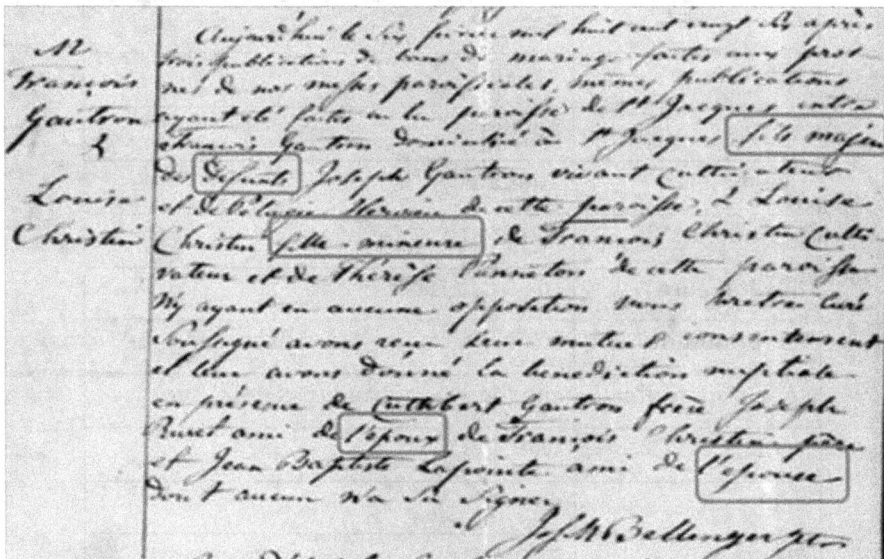

Figure 28-3: François is a *fils mineur*, or adult son. His father Joseph is *défunt*, or deceased. Louisa is a *fille mineure*; she is not of age. One of the witnesses, Joseph Buret, is the *ami de*, or friend of, *l'époux*, or the husband François. Jean Baptiste Lapointe is the friend of *l'épouse*, or the wife Louisa.

If either the groom's or the bride's father was deceased at the time of the marriage, one of two words appeared before his name: *feu* or *défunt*. If either the groom's or the bride's mother was deceased at the time of the marriage, you would see each of those words again, but with an added *e* at the end, *feue* or *défunte*.

If the groom had been married previous to the current marriage, the record would not list his parents. It would tell you that he was a *veuf*, or widower. If the bride had been previously married, she would be referred to as *veuve* for widow.

At the end of the document, the priest listed the witnesses who appeared on behalf of the groom and the bride, for example the father of the groom or the brother of the bride. The word for groom is *époux*; the word for bride is *épouse*. Sometimes, depending on the scribe's handwriting, it is difficult to distinguish between the final *x* on *époux* and the final *se* on *épouse*.

See figure 28-4 for gender clues in marriage records.

Gender clues in marriage records	
fils	son
fille	daughter
fils majeur	adult son
fille majeure	adult daughter
fils mineur	the groom is not of age
fille mineure	the bride is not of age
feu or défunt	the male referred to is deceased
feue or défunte	the female referred to is deceased
veuf	widower
veuve	widow
époux	husband
épouse	wife

Figure 28-4: Gender clues in marriage records

Clues in Burial Records

The wording in a burial record is very similar to that of a baptism record. Sometimes the priest recorded the event as "by we" (*par nous*), "the undersigned priest" (*prêtre soussigné*), "was buried" (*a eté inhumé*) [the name of the deceased] "in the cemetery . . . ." The French words for "was buried" are *a eté inhumé*. If *inhumé* ends in an *e accent aigu (é)*, then the deceased person is a male. If *inhumée* ends in an *e accent aigu* followed by another *e (ée)*, then the deceased is female (Figure 28-5).

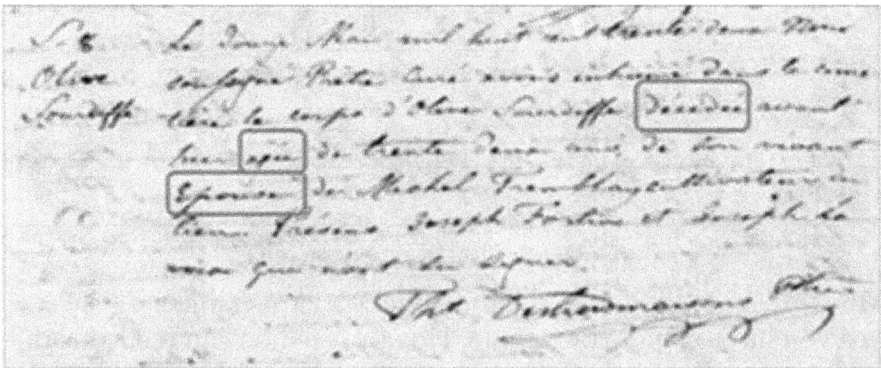

Figure 28-5: *Décédée* indicates a female died. *Agée de trente ans* means the female was 32 years old. She was the *épouse*, or wife, of Michel Tremblay.

Again look for the word *par* before *nous*. If there is no *par*, and all you see is *nous prêtre soussigné avons inhumé*, then the above does not apply. The word *inhumé* is not modifying the deceased. Instead it is also part of a verb phrase, ". . . we, the undersigned priest, . . . have buried . . . ."

Other clues in a burial record follow the deceased's name when the priest tells you the date and age of death (Figure 28-6). The priest may indicate a male's date of death as *décédé le sept d' avril* (died the 7th of April). The word for died or deceased is *décédé*. For a female there would be an extra *e* at the end, *décédée*. *Agé d'un mois* means the child was aged one month at time of death. Add an *e* to form *agée*, and you know the child is female.

In burial records you will often also find the words *époux* (husband) and *épouse* (wife) referring to the spouse left behind.

Gender clues in burial records

inhumé	"buried," when the deceased person is male (Some priests use *inhumé* for both males and females.)
inhumée	"buried," when the deceased person is female
décédé	the deceased person is male
décédée	the deceased person is female
agé	"aged," when referring to a male
agée	"aged," when referring to a female
époux	husband
épouse	wife

Figure 28-6: Gender clues in burial records

Most often you will already know whether the subject of the record you have is male or female. However, when the record is difficult to read, spotting these words may be the only clues you have.

29
Saint vs Sainte
vs St. vs St-

French-Canadian genealogists often ask the question, "Which is the correct way to write 'saint' in French?"

That's a great question. You'll often see it written one of several different ways: *Saint*, *Sainte*, *St.*, *Ste.*, *St-*, or *Ste-*. So under which circumstances would you use any or all of them?

We're really talking about two separate issues here: whether or not to use an *e*, and whether to use a period, a hyphen, or neither. Let's start with the *e* first.

St. or Ste.

In chapter 25, we discussed how nouns are classified as either masculine or feminine. An adjective that describes a feminine noun indicates the gender with the placement of an *e* at the end. So the adjective for "small" when describing a boy is *petit*, but for a girl it's *petite*. The same thing applies to the word "saint." When the saint is a male, we use *saint*. When the saint is a female, we use *sainte*. The abbreviations follow the same pattern: *St.* for a male saint; *Ste.* for a female saint. So we have *St. Joseph*, but *Ste. Marie*.

For the most part, the final *e* indicating gender did not carry over to America. You will see many St. Mary's churches which, in Québec, would be *Ste. Marie*.

Also remember that we do not pronounce the final consonant of a word unless there is an *e* at the end (see ch. 7). So for males, you will not hear the /t/ at the end of *saint*. In *St. Michel*, *St.* ends in a nasally /n/ sound (see ch. 17). An exception is if the following saint's name begins with a vowel, like *St. Antoine*. In this case, the *t* in *Saint* is linked with the initial vowel of the following word. This is called *liaison*, or linking, and you would pronounce the /t/. You will also hear the /t/ in *Ste. Marie* because of the final *e* in *Ste.*

Hyphens

The second issue deals with the use of hyphens versus today's practice of abbreviating "saint" with a period. There are two ways of dealing with this. Some believe that you should always write the name exactly the way it appears in the record. Most genealogy programs will allow you to write every name variation that you find. However, other genealogists make the personal decision to write place names without the hyphen. This conforms to the norms with which their audience would be familiar. You will see it written either way in published works, so I would suggest it's a matter of personal preference.

Online Indexes

Another problem occurs when looking up names beginning with "Saint" in online indexes. It was much easier when we scoured indexes located in the backs of books. We simply skimmed a couple of pages to see whether the publisher was recording the complete word *Saint* located alphabetically in the *sa-* section or the abbreviated version alphabetized in the *st-* section. It's not so easy when searching in a digitized index.

When searching in a native French database, you may have to search differently than you would in an English index. Since the PRDH is the leader, so to speak, of French-Canadian databases, I predict that in the future most native French databases will follow whatever standard they use. As of this writing, the PRDH uses no periods, hyphens, or spaces in surnames. The word *Saint* is not written out; it is abbreviated. To search for *St. George*, you would type in *stgeorge*. For *Ste. Marie*, you'd type *stemarie*. If you type in the entire word *Saint*, the results will bring up the abbreviated form of the word anyhow.

I checked on one of the more widely used census indexes here in America, HeritageQuest Online, for the surname St. George. In order to catch them all, you would have to do a search for St. George with "Saint" spelled *St.*, *St* (no period), and *Saint*. Again, for the surname Sainte Marie, usually in America the gender specific adjective did not carry over. However there *are* exceptions. Again in Heritage Quest Online, a search for Sainte Marie brought up two people with the spelling of *Sainte*. However there are *no* abbreviated *Saintes* spelled *Ste.* You will also find *St.* (yes, even though it's a female saint), *St* (no period), and *Saint* combined with Marie. So the census indexes for HeritageQuest Online need to be searched by the full name as well as the abbreviations spelled with and without the period.

In FamilySearch, a search for St. George produced the same results whether or not you used a period or a hyphen after St. However, you get different search results if you write out the word. So remember to search for both the full name and the abbreviated name with a period.

The best thing to do before researching a "Saint" name in a database is to do a test run. Type the name out with an *e* and without an *e*. Try it with and without periods, hyphens, and spaces. Then make a note of how that particular database handles these surnames for future searches; and remember that French-language databases and English-language databases may handle searches very differently.

30
Québec—the City
or the Province?

Did research on one of your ancestors uncover that he was from Quebec or moved to Quebec? Was he *de Québec* or *du Québec*? Did she move *à Québec* or *au Québec*? Were you confused? Did it mean the city of Quebec or the entire province of Quebec? There's a clue in the French.

Nouns in French have a gender assigned to them, even nouns that we consider gender-neutral in English, like "house." (For a review, see chapter 25.) In French, the word *maison*, or "house," is feminine. All adjectives describing it must also be in the feminine form. *La* is the feminine form for the word "the," so "the house" would be *la maison*.

The word for dog, *chien*, is masculine, so "the dog" would be *le chien*.

> *La maison*-both words in the feminine form
>
> *Le chien*-both words in the masculine form

Now let's combine those with two of the most common French prepositions, *à* and *de*. *À* is the word for *at* or *to*. *De* means *of* or *from*.

So "to the house" would translate as *à la maison*. "From the house" or "of the house" would be *de la maison*.

However, when the noun is masculine, there's a slight change. Because the word *chien* is masculine, in French, instead of saying *de le chien* for "of the dog," we change the *de le* to *du*. *Du chien*. Instead of *à le chien* for "to the dog," the French say *au chien* (Figure 30-1).

Preposition	Meaning	Feminine	Masculine
à	at, to	à la	à le = au
de	of, from	de la	de le = du

Figure 30-1: More prepositions with articles

What does this have to do with the place name Quebec? If referring to Quebec City, keep in mind that the city is a feminine noun. The province of Quebec is a masculine noun.

If you see *de Québec* or *à Québec*, then the writer is referring to the feminine word for the city. If you see *du Québec* or *au Québec*, then the writer is referring to the province (Figure 30-2).

	The city	The province
"at" or "to"	à Québec	au Québec
"of" or "from"	de Québec	du Québec

Figure 30-2: Proper preposition and article with Québec

Now you'll know if your search should take you to the city of Quebec, or if it encompasses the entire province. If your ancestor was *du Québec*, and you could not find him in the city of Quebec's parish registers, now you know why. You have an entire province left to hunt through.

Part 4
Making the Records Speak

Introduction to *Making the Records Speak*

Do you ever sit with a document in front of you and stare blankly at the French words? Do you imagine all the details of your French-Canadian ancestor's life that are hidden in those undecipherable sentences? If only you could completely pick out all the clues hidden in that document! Do you now regret taking that extra gym class instead of French 101?

In Part 4, you will learn some French genealogy words. These basics will help you to pick out those clues. Hopefully, it will be enough for you to understand the critical data located in the record.

The more effort you expend in memorizing the words up front, the faster it will be to translate the documents. As an alternative, you might decide to keep this reference handy to refer back to as needed.

However you decide to use this information, don't give up. You can do this!

31
Baptism, Marriage, and Burial Abbreviations

In America, we're used to searching for vital records: births, marriages, and deaths. When you first move from American records to Quebec records, you'll see the abbreviations *b*, *m*, and *s* in front of dates. Your initial inclination might be to associate those letters with birth, marriage, and … *s*? The big question mark sets in. What does the *s* stand for? The clue is in the fact that we are dealing with church records, not civil records.

Let's start with the *b*. It does not stand for "birth." The French word for "birth" is *naissance*, abbreviated with an *n*. Think of the word *renaissance*, which means "rebirth." The *b* stands for the French word *baptême*, which means "baptism." The *m* *does* stand for *mariage*, or "marriage." The French word for "death" is *décès*, abbreviated *d*. The *s* stands for *sépulture*, or "burial" (Figure 31-1).

Our French ancestors were not so much interested in vital records as the sacraments. The priests were more concerned with recording baptisms, marriages, and burials, although dates of births and deaths often appear in the original church records also.

So, remember, *n* for birth, *b* for baptism, *m* for marriage, *d* for death, and *s* for burial.

Church Record Abbreviations		
English	**French**	**Abbreviation**
birth	*naissance*	n
baptism	*baptême*	b
marriage	*mariage*	m
death	*décès*	d
burial	*sépulture*	s

Figure 31-1: Church record abbreviations

32
French Numbers

No matter whether you have a baptism, marriage, or burial record in front of you, the first line usually contains the date of the document.

To read dates, you have to be able to read numbers. Take some time to familiarize yourself with the spellings of these numbers. It will make your job of reading the dates much easier, especially when the writing is faded or a particular priest had very challenging handwriting. I cannot stress enough how important it is to be able to recognize these words for the numbers that they are. After we go over ways to remember the numbers, I will direct you to several websites that make it easier to become familiar with these words through practice.

To be able to read a date, you need to know the French words for the numbers up to 100 plus the number for 1000. It's easier to learn these by grouping them according to commonalities.

Step 1: Numbers 1–10

We're going to start with the numbers one through ten: one-*un*, two-*deux*, three-*trois*, four-*quatre*, five-*cinq*, six-*six*, seven-*sept*, eight-*huit*, nine-*neuf*, and ten-*dix*: *un, deux, trois, quatre, cinq, six, sept, huit, neuf, dix*. You don't need to know how to pronounce them, but you certainly need to recognize them and understand their value.

The following chart gives you the English number, the French number, and some clues (mnemonic devices) to help you remember each number (Figure 32-1).

English	French	Clue
one	*un*	Think unit, unite as one.
two	*deux*	Think deuce, double.
three	*trois*	Think trio, triplets.
four	*quatre*	A quarter is a 4th of a dollar; quadruplets.
five	*cinq*	Think quintuplets (*c* and *qu* are interchangeable).
six	*six*	'Nuf said.
seven	*sept*	Think septuplets.
eight	*huit*	No clue, but this one seems to be an easy one to remember nevertheless.
nine	*neuf*	Each begins with *n*.
ten	*dix*	Think digit; we have ten digits on our hands, and ten more on our feet.

Figure 32-1: Numbers 1-10

Step 2: Numbers 11–16

Once you have those memorized, it's time to learn the words for eleven through sixteen: eleven-*onze*, twelve-*douze*, thirteen-*treize*, fourteen-*quatorze*, fifteen-*quinze*, and sixteen-*seize* (Figure 32-2).

English	French	Clue
eleven	*onze*	Think the "on-" in one for the two ones in eleven.
twelve	*douze*	Think dozen.
thirteen	*treize*	Both begin with *t*.
fourteen	*quatorze*	Remember its relationship to *quatre*. *Quatre* = 4; *quatorze* = 14
fifteen	*quinze*	Think quintuplets again to remember the 5 in 15.
sixteen	*seize*	Both begin with *s*.

Figure 32-2: Numbers 11-16

Step 3: Numbers 17–19

If you know the single-digit numbers, then seventeen through nineteen are easy—just add 7, 8, and 9 to the number 10. Seventeen is basically ten plus seven, *dix-sept*; eighteen is ten plus eight, *dix-huit*; and nineteen is ten plus nine or *dix-neuf* (Figure 32-3).

English	French	Clue
seventeen	*dix-sept*	10 + 7
eighteen	*dix-huit*	10 + 8
nineteen	*dix-neuf*	10 + 9

Figure 32-3: Numbers 17-19

Step 4: The Decades (20, 30, 40, 50, 60)

The next step is to learn the decades: 20, 30, 40, 50, 60. Twenty is *vingt*; thirty-*trente*; forty-*quarante*; fifty-*cinquante*; sixty-*soixante*. You'll notice I stopped here before getting to 70, 80, and 90 because those decades get a little funky, at least compared to English (Figure 32-4).

English	French	Clue
twenty	vingt	An item is vintage after it is twenty years old.
thirty	trente	Both begin with t.
forty	quarante	There's that 4 again.
fifty	cinquante	Think cinq for 5.
sixty	soixante	Soix- is very close to six.

Figure 32-4: The decades

Step 5: The Funky Decades (70, 80, 90)

Instead of having a unique word for "seventy," the French use what amounts to "sixty plus ten," or *soixante-dix*.

You probably remember the first words of the Gettysburg Address, "Fourscore and seven years ago . . . ." A score equals twenty years, so fourscore is four groups of twenty years, or eighty years. And so it is in French. The word for "eighty" is basically four groups of twenty, *quatre-vingts*. The number "ninety" is four groups of twenty plus ten, *quatre-vingt-dix* (Figure 32-5).

English	French	Clue
seventy	soixante-dix	60 + 10
eighty	quatre-vingts	4 groups of 20
ninety	quatre-vingt-dix	4 groups of 20 + 10

Figure 32-5: The funky decades

Step 6: Decades Plus 1

Here is another example of how learning the lower numbers makes it easier to learn the higher numbers. For the numbers 21, 31, 41, 51, and 61, you simply add the French words for "and one," *et un*, after each decade. Twenty-one is *vingt et un*, followed by *trente et un, quarante et un, cinquante et un,* and *soixante et un* (Figure 32-6)

English	French	Clue
21	*vingt et un*	Twenty and one
31	*trente et un*	Thirty and one
41	*quarante et un*	Forty and one
51	*cinquante et un*	Fifty and one
61	*soixante et un*	Sixty and one

Figure 32-6: Decades plus 1

Step 7: Decades Plus Singles

The numbers in between are formed with the decade number followed by a hyphen and the single digit number. So "twenty-two" is *vingt-deux*; followed by *vingt-trois*, "twenty-three"; *vingt-quatre*, "twenty-four"; and so on up to *vingt-neuf*, "twenty-nine." After *trente*, "thirty"; and *trente et un*, "thirty-one"; you have *trente-deux*, *trente-trois*, up to *trente-neuf*. *Quarante-cinq* is "forty-five"; *cinquante-sept* is "fifty-seven"; *soixante-six* is "sixty-six" (Figure 32-7)

English	French	Clue
22	*vingt-deux*	Twenty two
33	*trente-trois*	Thirty three
44	*quarante-quatre*	Forty four
55	*cinquante-cinq*	Fifty five
66	*soixante-six*	Sixty six

Figure 32-7: Decades plus singles

Step 8: Funky Decades Plus Singles

The French word for "seventy" equates to sixty and ten, or *soixante-dix*. The number "seventy-one" is sixty plus eleven, or *soixante-et-onze*.

For the rest of the numbers in the 70s, add the French numbers *douze* through *dix-neuf* to the number seventy, *soixante-dix*, to form seventy-two through seventy-nine. So we have *soixante-douze* (sixty plus twelve) for seventy-two; *soixante-treize* (sixty plus thirteen) for seventy-three; up to *soixante dix-neuf* (sixty plus nineteen) for seventy-nine.

Eighty is four groups of twenty, or *quatre-vingts*. The numbers eighty-one through ninety-nine become four groups of twenty plus one all the way to four groups of twenty plus nineteen: *quatre-vingt-un* (eighty-one), *quatre-vingt-duex* (eighty-two), *quatre-vingt-dix* (four groups of twenty plus ten, or ninety), *quatre-vingt-dix-neuf* (four groups of twenty plus nineteen, or ninety-nine) (Figure 32-8)

English	French	Clue
71	*soixante-et-onze*	60 + 11
72	*soixante-douze*	60 + 12
79	*soixante-dix-neuf*	60 + 19
81	*quatre-vingt-un*	4 groups of 20 plus 1
88	*quatre-vingt-huit*	4 groups of 20 plus 8
91	*quatre-vingt-onze*	4 groups of 20 plus 11
99	*quatre-vingt-dix-neuf*	4 groups of 20 plus 19

Figure 32-8: Funky decades plus singles

Step 9: Numbers 100 and 1,000

The only other French numbers you need to read dates are the words for "one hundred," *cent* (think "century"); "one thousand," *mil* or *mille* (think "millennium"); and ordinal numbers, which are covered in chapter 33 (Figure 32-9).

English	French	Clue
100	*cent*	Think century.
1000	*mil, mille*	Think millenium.

Figure 32-9: Numbers 100 and 1,000

Legacy Dates

In some of the older records, you will occasionally see a date recorded with an alternate term for the numbers seventy, eighty, or ninety (Figure 32-10).

Number	Legacy French
70	*septante*
80	*huitante, octante*
90	*nonante*

Figure 32-10: Legacy dates

Practice

I recommend you practice using the following websites. If any of these sites become obsolete, just search online for "French numbers." For a chart of French numbers, go to the Woodward French website[33] and scroll to the bottom.

At the *French Language Blog*[34] you can find all the numbers from 0 to 100 so you can familiarize yourself with the spellings.

At Quizlet[35] you can find a number of tools to help you learn *French Numbers 1–100*. And yes, it's going to seem like you've gone back to elementary school. But even as adults, some of these repetitive methods like flashcards are very useful. At the Quizlet.com website, you can practice your pronunciation with flashcards, practice your spelling of the words, quiz yourself, or play a couple of recognition games. The flashcards allow you to see the French and you give the English, or vice versa. It also allows you to practice the numbers sequentially or in random order as you become more advanced.

Once you think you know all the numbers from zero to 100, you can also practice at Rocket Languages' *French numbers*[36] . You

---

[33] http://www.woodwardfrench.com/lesson/numbers-from-1-to-100-in-french
[34] http://blogs.transparent.com/french/french-numbers-1-100
[35] http://quizlet.com/996950/french-numbers-1-100-flash-cards
[36] https://www.rocketlanguages.com/french/lessons/french-numbers

can listen to the pronunciation of each number and practice saying it yourself. Scroll to the bottom and you can test yourself with random numbers.

There you have several ways to practice depending upon your own likes and style. The more time you spend here before moving on, the easier it will be to translate French dates from memory. That will save you quite a bit of time.

Online Tools for Chapter 32

Woodward French-scroll down for a chart of French numbers
(https://www.woodwardfrench.com/lesson/numbers-from-1-to-100-in-french/)

French Language Blog-list of all numbers from 1-100
(http://blogs.transparent.com/french/french-numbers-1-100)

Quizlet's **French Numbers 1-100**-several practice activities
(http://quizlet.com/996950/french-numbers-1-100-flash-cards)

Rocket Languages' **French numbers**-practice your pronunciation
(https://www.rocketlanguages.com/french/lessons/french-numbers)

33
Ordinal Numbers

There are a few instances when you might come across ordinal numbers in French-Canadian records. Among others, the priest might use an ordinal number to describe the dates on which banns were read or to designate the degree of affinity or consanguinity.

Below is a marriage record (Figure 33-1) which states, *"Après la publication des trois bans de mariage faite le premier, quinzième et vingt deuxième du mois d'aoust."* This means, "After the publication of three bans of marriage made the first, fifteenth, and twenty-second day of the month of August." *Premier,*

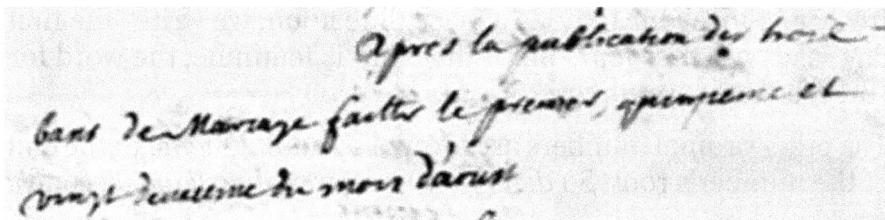

Figure 33-1: Ordinal numbers in a marriage record

quinzième, and *vingt-deuxième,* "first, fifteenth, and twenty-second," are ordinal numbers.

This next record states that the first bann was read *le premier jour de Janvier,* or "the first day of January." But notice that *premier* was abbreviated to a *1* followed by a superscript *er* (Figure 33-2).

Figure 33-2: Ordinal numbers in a marriage record

The record below states that there was a dispensation of the *premier degré d'affinité,* or the "first degree of affinity" (Figure 33-3).

Figure 33-3: Ordinal numbers in a marriage record

This next dispensation was due to the *quatrième degré de consanguinité,* or the "fourth degree of consanguinity" (Figure 33-4)

Figure 33-4: Ordinal numbers in a marriage record

It helps to be able to recognize these words. There are no more than thirty-one days in a month, so the French equivalent of "thirty-first" should be the highest ordinal number you need to know.

For the most part, ordinal numbers are formed exactly the same way, except for the first one. We construct the French word for "first," *premier,* differently than the rest. Its form must agree with the gender of the noun it is describing. (See chapter 25 for a refresher.) Since *jour* (day) is a masculine noun, we write "the first day" as *le premier jour.* But if the noun is feminine, the word for "first" becomes *première.*

The other ordinal numbers are formed by adding *-ième* to the end of the number's root. So *deux* (two) becomes *duexième* (second).

French Ordinal Numbers

Cardinal number	Ordinal number	Meaning
Un (m.)	Premier (m.)	First (m.)
Une (f.)	Première (f.)	First (f.)
Deux	Deuxième	Second
Trois	Troisième	Third
Quatre	Quatrième	Fourth
Cinq	Cinquième	Fifth
Six	Sixième	Sixth
Sept	Septième	Seventh
Huit	Huitième	Eighth
Neuf	Neuvième	Ninth
Dix	Dixième	Tenth
Onze	Onzième	Eleventh
Douze	Douzième	Twelfth
Treize	Treizième	Thirteenth
Quatorze	Quatorzième	Fourteenth
Quinze	Quinzième	Fifteenth
Seize	Seizième	Sixteenth
Dix-sept	Dix-septième	Seventeenth
Dix-huit	Dix-huitième	Eighteenth
Dix-neuf	Dix-neuvième	Nineteenth
Vingt	Vingtième	Twentieth
Vingt-et-un	Vingt-et-unième	Twenty-first
Vingt-deux	Vingt-deuxième	Twenty-second
Vingt-trois	Vingt-troisième	Twenty-third
Vingt-quatre	Vingt-quatrième	Twenty-fourth
Vingt-cinq	Vingt-cinquième	Twenty-fifth
Vingt-six	Vingt-sixième	Twenty-sixth
Vingt-sept	Vingt-septième	Twenty-seventh
Vingt-huit	Vingt-huitième	Twenty-eighth
Vingt-neuf	Vingt-neuvième	Twenty-ninth
Trente	Trentième	Thirtieth
Trente-et-un	Trente-et-unième	Thirty-first

Figure 33-5: French ordinal numbers

See the chart (Figure 33-5) for ordinal numbers up to thirty-one, the largest number representing a day of the month.

Now that you're adept at reading ordinal numbers, you're ready to tackle the records, right? Not quite. Just when you think you have a handle on it, you'll find an ordinal number written as an abbreviation; and just to make it even trickier, there are several different ways to write those abbreviations.

Let's start with the word for "first," since that one is constructed differently from the rest.

If the word *premier* is used to describe a masculine noun, you'll usually see the abbreviation as the numeral *1* followed by a superscript *er*,

1st	*premier, unième*	1e, 1er, 1me
2nd	*deuxième*	2e, 2me
3rd	*troisième*	3e, 3me

Figure 33-6 Examples of ordinal number abbreviations

or *1er* (Figure 33-6). You abbreviate the feminine form (with an *e* at the end) as *1* followed by either a superscript *re*, a superscript *e*, or a superscript *ère* (*1re*, *1e*, or *1ère*).

You abbreviate the other ordinal numbers, which all end in *ième*, by following the numeral, for example *2*, with either a superscript *e, me, ème*, or *è* (*2e, 2me, 2ème*, or *2^è*). However, there are spelling changes for *quatrième, cinquième* and *neuvième*. Note the missing *e* after the *r* in *quatrième*, the added *u* after the *q* in *cinquième*; and the change from *f* to *v* in *neuvième*.

70th	septantième
80th	huitantième, octantième
90th	nonantième

Figure 33-7: Legacy ordinal numbers

Remember the alternate spellings for the numbers seventy, eighty, and ninety from chapter 32? Figure 33-7 shows how to change those to cardinal numbers also.

One other thing you might occasionally see are Roman numerals in place of the Arabic ordinal numbers. Quebec was settled in the 17th century. In French, "seventeen" is *dix-sept*; so 17th is *dix-septième*. The Roman numeral would be written as *XVII* followed by a superscript *e* (*XVIIe*) (Figure 33-8).

Ordinal Number Abbreviations

Premier (m.)	1er
Première	1re, 1e, 1ère
Deuxième	2e, 2me, 2ème, 2^{è}
Quinzième	15e, 15me, 15ème, 15^{è}
Seventeenth	XVIIe
Eighteenth	XVIIIe
Nineteenth	XIXe

Figure 33-8: Ordinal number abbreviations

The burial record for Marie Catherine Sourdive begins differently than most records (Figure 33-9). Instead of beginning with the year, it begins with the date written as an ordinal number. Can you figure out the date? (see Appendix C for the answer.)

Now hopefully, if you run across any of these numbers in a French record, you'll recognize them more easily.

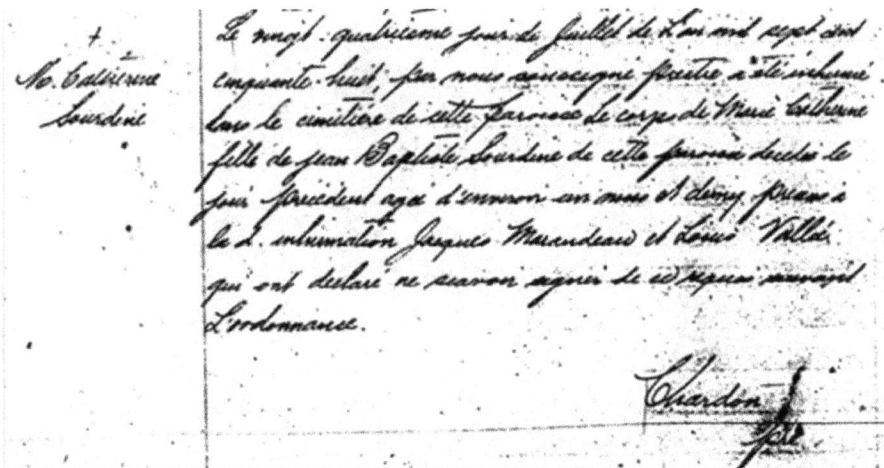

Figure 33-9: Burial record for Marie Catherine Sourdive

34
French Dates

Now that you're familiar with French cardinal and ordinal numbers, it's now time to look at the words for the months: *janvier, février, mars, avril, mai, juin, juillet, août, septembre, octobre, novembre, décembre* (Figure 34-1). Note that the French do not capitalize the names of the months.

Caution

Unless the handwriting is extremely clear, it is easy to mix up the French words for March and May (*mars* and *mai*) as well as the two words for April and August (*avril* and *août*). If you're not sure which month it is, check the entries before and after to see if you can figure out which one would come chronologically.

Abbreviations

Today, September through December are the ninth through the twelfth months. In Roman times, there were only ten months in the calendar year. September was the seventh, which is why its root, *sept*, comes from the Latin word for "seven." The root *octo* in October comes from the Latin word for "eight"; November comes from *novem*, the word for "nine"; and the root in December, *decem*, means "ten."

The priests, well-versed in Latin, abbreviated September with the numeral seven followed by a superscript *-bre* (Ex: 7*bre*). These are the last three letters in the French words for September, October, November, and December. October was *8bre*; November *9bre*; and December either the number *10* or the Roman numeral *X* followed by the superscript *-bre*.

French Months	
January	*janvier*
February	*février*
March	*mars*
April	*avril*
May	*mai*
June	*juin*
July	*juillet*
August	*août*
September	*septembre*
October	*octobre*
November	*novembre*
December	*décembre*

Figure 34-1: French months

Examples

A typical date in a baptism record might be *le dix-sept avril mil huit cent soixante-quatorze.*

That translates to "the seventeenth of April 1874."

> *le dix-sept avril* = the seventeenth of April
>
> *mil huit cent* = eighteen hundred
>
> *soixante-quatorze* = seventy-four

Practice

Can you apply what you've learned? Use your knowledge of French numbers (chapter 32) and French dates (this chapter) to determine the following dates. You'll find the answers in Appendix C.

1) Le quinze novembre mil sept cent cinquante neuf

2) Le douze août mil huit cent soixante sept

3) Le vingt cinq juin mil sept cent quatre vingt six

35
Family Relations

An experienced genealogist knows to look for clues to extended family in a document's witnesses. Sometimes you can discover people with a similar surname. Then you only have to figure out the relationship. But that's not always easy to do.

Often in French-Canadian documents, the godparents or witnesses include family or friends of the couple. You should consider yourself extremely fortunate when the document also lists the exact relationship.

In a baptism record you will occasionally find the relationship of the godparents to the child. A marriage record lists witnesses at the end of the record. It begins with members of the groom's family followed by those of the bride. Often you will find the relationship of those witnesses to the bride or groom. If the witnesses to a burial are family members, their relationship might also be given.

Notarial records give clues also. For example, in a land sale, the notary will often mention the relationship between grantor and grantee if they are family members.

The clues are there; you just have to spot them. When you do, you'll be able to piece together your French-Canadian family.

Let's take a look at the French words for different family relationships, beginning with the immediate family, or *famille*. The charts that follow are grouped for ease of use by type of family relationship: parents, siblings, grandparents and beyond, the younger generation, couples, other relatives, and godrelatives (my new made-up word).

You might already be familiar with the words for the nuclear family: *père* for "father," *mère* for "mother," *frère* for "brother," and *soeur* for "sister." If the dad is really the stepdad, he's known as the *beau-père*. However *beau-père* can also be "father-in-law." So you may have to chart out the complete family before you can determine which one is correct. Similarly, your stepmother would be your *belle-mère*. But *belle-mère* can also be "mother-in-law." Another word for both "stepmother" and "mother-in-law" is *marâtre*. A "foster father" is a *père nourricier* (Figure 35-1).

Parents (*les parents*)		
French	**English**	**Notes**
Père	Father	
Mère	Mother	
Beau-père	Stepfather	Use records to determine precise relationship.
Beau-père	Father-in-law	
Belle-mère	Stepmother	Use records to determine precise relationship.
Belle-mère	Mother-in-law	
Marâtre	Stepmother	Use records to determine precise relationship.
Marâtre	Mother-in-law	
Père nourricier	Foster father	

Figure 35-1: French words for parental relationships

Similarly your brother-in-law or step-brother would both be known as your *beau-frère*; and your sister-in-law or stepsister would be known as your *belle-soeur* (*belle* is the feminine form of *beau*). There are several other fraternal and sororal designations, such as *frère de lait* for "foster brother" and specifically *frère germain* or *soeur germaine* (note the *e* on the end indicating female) for brothers or sisters by the same mother and father. There are specific terms for both brothers and sisters who share only one parent. *Frère consanguin* (related to the word "consanguinity," meaning "by blood") or *soeur consanguine* indicates a brother or sister by the same father but a different mother. Another way to say it is *frère de père seulement,* or "brother by father only."

If brothers or sisters share the same mother, they would be a *frère utérin* or *soeur utérine,* brother or sister by the same mother but a different father. Think of *in utero.* An alternate way is *frère de mère seulement,* "brother by the mother only," or half-brother sharing a mother (Figure 35-2).

Siblings (*les frères et soeurs*)		
French	**English**	**Notes**
Frère	Brother	
Sœur	Sister	
Beau-frère	Stepbrother	Use records to detemine precise relationship.
Beau-frère	Brother-in-law	
Belle-sœur	Stepsister	Use records to determine precise relationship.
Belle-sœur	Sister-in-law	
Frère de lait	Foster brother	
Frère germain	Brother with same mother and father	
Sœur germaine	Sister with same mother and father	
Frère consanguin	Brother by same father, different mother	Related to 'consanguinity,' by blood
Frère de père seulement	Brother by same father, different mother	
Sœur consanguine	Sister by same father, different mother	Related to 'consanguinity,' by blood

Siblings (*les frères et soeurs*)		
French	**English**	**Notes**
Soeur de père seulement	Sister by same father, different mother	
Frère utérin	Brother by same mother, different father	Think of 'in utero'
Frère de mère seulement	Brother by same mother, different father	
Soeur utérine	Sister by same mother, different father	Think of 'in utero'
Soeur de mère seulement	Sister by same mother, different father	

Figure 35-2: French words for sibling relationships

Let's back up now to the earlier generations. A grandfather could be both your *grandpère* or *aïeul*. Your grandmother would be your *grand-mère* or your *aïeule*. A great-grandfather is a *bisaïeul*, and a great-grandmother is a *bisaïeule*. A great-great-grandfather is a *trisaïeul*, and a great- great-grandmother is a *trisaïeule* (bi- for two generations back, and tri- for three generations back) (Figure 35-3).

Grandparents have grandchildren. A grandson is a *petit-fils*, and a granddaughter is a *petite-fille*. A great-grandson or a great-granddaughter would have the word *arrière* before it, *arrière-petit-fils* or *arrière-petite-fille*. *Arrière* before the word "grandfather" or "grandmother" indicates "great-grandfather" or "great-grandmother."

Any baby or child is called an *enfant*. As we learned in an earlier chapter, *fils* is "son" and *fille* is "daughter." So your stepson or your son-in-law would be your *beau-fils*. Your stepdaughter or daughter-in-law would be your *belle-fille*. Another word for "son-in-law" is *gendre* (Figure 35-4).

There are many terms used to describe a couple who is married or about to be married. Since English borrowed these words from

Elders (*les ainés*)

French	English
Grandpère	Grandfather
Aïeul	Grandfather
Grandmère	Grandmother
Aïeule	Grandmother
Bisaïeul	Great-grandfather
Arrière-grand-père	Great-grandfather
Bisaïeule	Great-grandmother
Arrière-grand-mère	Great-grandmother
Trisaïeul	Great-great-grandfather
Trisaïeule	Great-great-grandmother

Figure 35-3: French words for elder relationships

Youngsters (*les jeunes*)

French	English	Notes
Enfant	Baby, child	
Fils	Son	
Fille	Daughter	
Petit-fils	Grandson	
Petite-fille	Granddaughter	
Arrière-petit-fils	Great-grandson	
Arrière-petite-fille	Great-granddaughter	
Beau-fils	Stepson	Use records to determine precise relationship.
Beau-fils	Son-in-law	
Gendre	Son-in-law	
Belle-fille	Stepdaughter	Use records to determineprecise relationship.
Belle-fille	Daughter-in-law	

Figure 35-4: French words for relationships with children

French, everyone knows that a *fiancé* for the men and *fiancée* for the females refer to an engaged or betrothed couple. *Mari* means "husband." *Marié* means "groom" or "husband," and *mariée* means "bride" or "wife." The word *femme* can mean "woman"; but it also can indicate marital status referring to "wife." The other two words often found in church records are *époux* for "husband" and *épouse* for "wife" (Figure 35-5).

Couples (*le couple*)		
French	**English**	**Notes**
Fiancé	Betrothed	Male
Fiancée	Betrothed	Female
Mari	Husband	
Femme	Wife, woman	
Marié	Groom, husband	Male
Mariée	Bride, wife	Female
Époux	Husband	
Épouse	Wife	

Figure 35-5: French words for couple relationships

Now we'll take a quick look at extended family (Figure 35-6). Your uncle and aunt would be your *oncle* and *tante*. How many of us have either an *Oncle* Joseph or a *Tante* Marie? Their son would be your *cousin*. Add an *e* to the end, and their daughter would be your *cousine*. *Cousin germain* or *cousine germaine* specifically refer to first cousins. Your siblings' children would be your nieces and nephews. Niece in French is *nièce*, and nephew is *neveu*.

Extended family (*parente*)		
French	**English**	**Notes**
Oncle	Uncle	
Tante	Aunt	
Cousin	Cousin	Male
Cousine	Cousine	Female
Cousin germain	First cousin	Male
Cousine germaine	First cousin	Female
Nièce	Niece	
Neveu	Nephew	

Figure 35-6: French words for extended family

Godrelatives	
French	**English**
Parrain	Godfather
Marraine	Godmother
Filleul	Godson
Filleule	Goddaughter

Figure 35-7: French words for godrelatives

Every baptism ends with the godparents' names. The godfather is the *parrain*, and the godmother is the *marraine*. Their godson is a *filleul*, and their goddaughter is a *filleule* (Figure 35-7).

That should cover most of the family relationships you'll find in either church records or notarial records. You should now be able to accurately place new people in your family tree.

36
Relationship Clues

Are you struggling to research Quebec records because you've never taken a French class in your life? The first step in researching your French-Canadian ancestry is the ability to pick out crucial information in each record—the names, dates, and places. The next step is to differentiate the nuances. Hidden in these nuances are the clues you need to determine connections or to fill in crucial details in your ancestors' lives.

We covered family relation words in chapter 35. Now let's take a look at some other words you'll encounter, beginning with words referring to the children.

The Children

In chapter 25, we learned about masculine and feminine nouns. Often a masculine noun becomes feminine by adding an *e* to the end. So it is with the word for *born*.

Né indicates a male was born. Add an *e* to the end and it refers to a female. *Illégitime* refers to a child who is illegitimate, as opposed to one who is *légitime*. If a child is referred to as *naturel*, it *can* mean he is illegitimate, but not always. In such cases, the child might take the surname of the mother, or the surname would be *inconnu*, or unknown (Figure 36-1).

The Children	
né (m)	born
née (f)	born
illégitime	illegitimate
légitime	legitimate
naturel	illegitimate (not always)
inconnu(e)	unknown
ondoyé(e)	baptized provisionally
enfant	baby, child
enfant exposé	foundling
enfant trouvé	foundling
orphelin(e)	orphan
jumeaux	twins (two boys or boy and girl)
jumelles	twins (two girls)
mort né	stillborn

Figure 36-1: French words for children

If you see the word *ondoyé* (or *ondoyée* for females), it means that the child was baptized provisionally. This would occur when there was fear that the child would die before making it to the church for a formal service. The baptism was usually performed by the midwife or the father.

An *enfant* is a baby or child. An *enfant exposé* or an *enfant trouvé* is a foundling, and the male *orphelin* or female *orpheline* is an orphan. Many families had twins. The word *jumeaux* indicates that the twins consisted of either two males or one male and one female. *Jumelles* meant both children were girls. *Mort né* (born dead) indicates a stillbirth.

Age Indicators

There are several terms used to describe the youngsters and the senior members of the family (Figure 36-2). *Jeune* can mean "junior" or "the younger." A *garçon* is a boy or an unmarried young man. If a child is in his or her *minorité*, or minority, then he is a *mineur*, or minor, for a male and *mineure* for a girl. This means they were under legal age, which was twenty-five during

Age Indicators	
jeune	junior, the younger
garçon	boy, unmarried young man
minorité	minority, under legal age
mineur(e)	minor, younger, under legal age
petit(e)	small, little
petit frère	little brother
homme	man
l'aînè	the older, senior
majeur(e)	of legal age, older
vieux (m)	old
vielle (f)	old
plus âgé(e)	older, oldest, elder, eldest
plus vieux	older, oldest, elder, eldest
feu(e)	deceased
défunt(e)	deceased

Figure 36-2: French words indicating age/condition

most of the French regime. The word *petit* can mean "small" or "little," but in the phrase *son petit frère*, it means "his little brother."

When that *garçon* grows into an *homme*, or man, he might become *l'aîné*, the "older" or "senior." If he's reached the age of majority he is now referred to as *majeur*, or *majeure* for females. A male becomes *vieux*, or old, and a female becomes *vielle*. If he is either older, the oldest, the elder, or the eldest, he is *plus âgé*, or *âgée* for females, or *plus vieux*.

Finally at the end of life, a man is *feu* or *défunt*, or "deceased" (*feue* or *défunte* for females).

Marital Status

Several words in French, as in English, have more than one meaning, depending on the context (Figure 36-3). Such a word is *garçon*, which can indicate age or marital status. It not only is the word for "boy," but also "an unmarried young man." If he is a bachelor, he is *célibataire*, or he is a *vieux garçon. Seul* and *seule* tell us the person is single or alone (think "solo"). So an *homme seul* is a single man and a *femme seule* is a single woman.

Continuing with the women, a *mademoiselle* is a miss or an unmarried woman, as is a *vierge* (think "virgin"). If you've been a *mademoiselle* for a few too many years, you become a spinster, or *fileuse*.

Once a couple marries, they are *mariés*. Women in Quebec used their maiden names throughout life. Once living in the United States, they mostly adopted the American custom of taking on the husband's surname. You might see them referred to as Jeanne

Marital Status	
garçon	boy, unmarried young man
célibataire	bachelor, single, unmarried
vieux garçon	bachelor
seul(e)	single, alone
homme seul	single man
femme seule	single woman
mademoiselle	Miss, unmarried woman
vierge	unmarried woman
fileuse	spinster
mariés	married
née	followed by maiden name (ex : Jeanne Paquet *née* Bouchard = Jeanne Paquet born Bouchard)
veuf (m)	widower
veuve (f)	widow

Figure 36-3: French words indicating marital status

Paquet *née* Bouchard, meaning Jeanne Paquet "born" Bouchard. From this we know that Jeanne's maiden name is Bouchard, and she married Mr. Paquet.

Once a spouse has died, a man becomes a widower, or *veuf*; a woman becomes a widow, or *veuve*.

Economic Status

If a man is a member of the *noblesse*, or "nobility," he is a *noble* or nobleman. The *petite noblesse* refers to "the gentry," a higher social class but below the nobility (Figure 36-4).

Economic Status	
noble	nobleman
noblesse	nobility
petite noblesse	gentry

Figure 36-4: French words describing economic status

Titles

Most people are familiar with the three most common titles of address in French: *Monsieur, Mademoiselle*, and *Madame. Monsieur* means "Mr." or "Sir" and is abbreviated as capital *M*. The abbreviation for *Mademoiselle* (Miss) is *Mlle. Madame*, meaning "Mrs.," is abbreviated *Mme*. One other title, *demoiselle*, is translated as "Miss" and can refer to a single woman from a well-to-do family or a married woman (Figure 36-5).

Titles of Address & Abbreviations		
Monsieur	M.	Mr., sir
Demoiselle		Miss (of well-to-do parents; may refer to a married woman also)
Mademoiselle	Mlle.	Miss, an unmarried woman
Madame	Mme.	Mrs.

Figure 36-5: French words for titles of address with abbreviations

Association with Family

If someone is not at all familiar with a family, then he is an *étranger*, or stranger. The word can also mean "foreign" or "foreigner." Many marriage records are signed by friends, noted as *ami* for male friends and *amie* for females. Each is a *témoin*, or witness. A *proche parent* is a close relative. The mid-

Association with Family	
étranger	foreigner, foreign, stranger
ami(e)	friend
proche parent	close relative
sage-femme	midwife
témoin	witness
tuteur	guardian

Figure 36-6: French words for family associations

wife, or *sage-femme*, would be present at the birth. And finally, some records appoint a guardian, or *tuteur* (Figure 36-6).

Now go back through your church records and notary records. Look for these words. Do they clarify family relationships for you?

37
Clues to Nationality

When are your French not French? When they're English, Spanish, Italian, or German of course!

Not all of our French Canadian ancestors actually emigrated from France. A few came from other countries, usually Catholic countries in Europe.

Dit names (see chapter 25) sometimes became surnames and give you clues to your ancestors' origins. Sometimes an ancestor's country of origin may appear in a record, but the document records the French spelling of that country. Would you recognize it for what it is? It helps to know the French names for these proper nouns and proper adjectives so you can spot them when they occur in the records.

As a review, a proper noun would be, for example, the name of a particular country, like Spain. A proper adjective is a variation of that word that we use to describe an item or a person from that country, like Spanish. It helps to be able to recognize either form of the word in French.

For an example, let's look at the baptism of a baby, Romaine Robideau, in Québec in 1669 (Figure 37-1; this and the following records are from Drouin Institute, *Québec Records*, www.geneal-ogiequebec.com). Her father is André Robideau dit l'Espagnol. Realizing that *l'Espagnol* is French for "the Spaniard," you now have a very good clue as to where to look for records from his earlier life. Sure enough, on his marriage record from 1667, his home parish is listed as Ste. Marie in *Espagne*, the French word for "Spain" (Figure 37-2).

Baptism	1669-07-11
Québec	Birth : 1669-07-11
	Drouin Collection record :
	d1p_31410593.jpg
ROBIDEAU , ROMAINE	sex
Subject	f.
ROBIDEAU LESPAGNOL , ANDRE	
Father	

Figure 37-1: dit l'Espagnol

Marriage	1667-06-07
Québec	Drouin Collection record :
	d1p_31410495.jpg
ROBIDOU , ANDRE	Mar. st.
Subject	single
Origin : STE-MARIE, ESPAGNE	

Figure 37-2: Original parish for André Robidou dit l'Espagnol

You might be thinking, "But that's easy. I can tell that *l'Espagnol* and *Espagne* refer to Spain. But if you've never learned a Romance language before, then the next one may be a bit more difficult.

André Spénard married Marie Charlotte Arnaud in Québec in 1690. He is *Allemand* from *Allemagne*. *Allemagne* is French for

Marriage	1690-04-05
Québec	Drouin Collection record : d1p_31411085.jpg

| SPINARD , ANDRE
Subject
Origin : ALLEMAND DE NATION | Mar. st.
single |

Figure 37-3: German origins

the country of Germany. He is *Allemand*, or German (Figure 37-3).

Perhaps the most well-known person from Nouvelle France carrying a nationality around as his *dit* name is Abraham Martin *dit l'Ecossais*, or Abraham Martin the Scotsman. Debate has been ongoing as to how he received this nickname, because it appears he was born in France in 1589. Did he travel to Scotland often? Did he live in Scotland for a while? In 2013 the Ontario Genealogical Society published an article[37] extending their theory based on research conducted by one of its members.

One of the most prevalent of these nationality *dit* names is *Langlais* or *Langlois*, "the Englishman." This often became the *dit* name for captives from the American colonies carried to Canada, such as the Reeves, the Otises, or the Webbers.

If you do a search in any French-Canadian database, you will also find many people with the surname *L'Italien*, or "the Italian" (Figure 37-4)

Num.	date	type	Parish	role	sex	standard name	standard first name
73157	1703-10-07	s	Hôtel-Dieu de Québec	subject	m	nicolas litalien	andre
246451	1755-10-12	b	Québec	father	m	letoile litalien	bonaventure
252472	1757-10-12	s	Québec	father	m	letoile litalien	bonaventure

Figure 37-4: Italian origins

There is also a deceased wife by the name of Solyme *Allemagne*, or Solyme Germany. Whenever you see any of these proper nouns

---

[37] https://familysearch.org/photos/artifacts/1749231

or proper adjectives appended to your ancestor's name, be sure to follow up on that clue.

The following table (Figure 37-5) shows the common proper nouns and proper adjectives that indicate nationality.

Nationality Clues			
Nouns		**Adjectives**	
l'Allemagne	Germany	*allemand*	German
l'Angleterre	England	*anglais*	English
l'Écosse	Scotland	*écossais*	Scottish
l'Espagne	Spain	*espagnol*	Spanish
la France	France	*français*	French
l'Italie	Italy	*italien*	Italian
le Portugal	Portugal	*portugais*	Portuguese

Figure 37-5: Nationality clues

38
Religious Denominations

In census records and other French-Canadian documents, you'll find mention of the various religious denominations. We find individual columns on the provincial censuses of 1831 and 1842 for entering denominational information. A number in each column tells us the number of people in the household belonging to that faith. In the 1851 and 1861 censuses, there is one column for religion. The enumerator had to write in the denomination for each person.

Let's take a look at the French words for those denominations. Luckily for Anglophones, in most cases the French word for the religion resembles the English word. Whether it is in the census or in some other written document, these are the words you'll need to recognize. We'll begin with the religions found in the columns of the 1831 census.

Most of our ancestors belonged to the Roman Catholic Church and are designated as *Catholique romain*. Sometimes you will see the abbreviation *R* or *ROM* for *romain*.

The French word for "church" is *église*. *l'Église d'Angleterre* means the person belonged to the Church of England. If a person belonged to *l'Église d'Écosse*, then he was a member of the Church of Scotland.

Many of the French words resemble their English counterparts. It's easy to recognize *Méthodiste* for "Methodist," *Presbytérien* for "Presbyterian," *Congrégationaliste* for "Congregationalist," and *Baptiste* for "Baptist." You will also see *Juif* for "Jew."

In the 1842 census, our Roman Catholic ancestors belong to *l'Église de Rome*, or "the church of Rome." Besides the Church of England, the Church of Scotland, Methodists, Presbyterians, Congregationalists, Baptists, and the Jews, there are several new columns.

Wesleyan Methodists could be members of either the British or Canadian sect, differentiated as *méthodistes wesleyens britanniques* or *méthodistes wesleyens canadiens*. The words for "Episcopal Methodists" are *méthodistes épiscopaux*. *Anabaptiste* means "Anabaptist," and *luthérien* indicates "Lutheran." The word for "Quakers" is spelled exactly the same, as are "Tunkers."[38] The French word for "Moravians" is *moraviens*. Finally, *l'Église réformée de la Hollande* (or Holland) indicates a member of the Dutch Reformed Church.

Instead of writing out the religion, some census records use an abbreviation. In the chart on the next page (Figure 38-1) is each religion mentioned in the 1831 and 1842 censuses in French and English, as well as its abbreviation.[39]

[38] According to the Catholic Encyclopedia, Tunkers are "a Protestant sect thus named from its distinctive baptismal rite. They are also called Dunkards, Dunkers, Brethren, and German Baptists."
[39] Abbreviations are from the Ontario GenWeb Census Project website at http://geneofun.on.ca/ontariocensus/faq-religion.html

Religious Denominations in the 1831 and 1842 Canadian Censuses

French	English	Abbreviation
Catholique romain or l'Église de Rome	Roman Catholic	RC
l'Église d'Angleterre	Church of England	CE
l'Église d'Écosse	Church of Scotland	CS
Méthodiste	Methodist	M
Presbytérien	Presbyterian	P
Congrégationaliste	Congregationalist	CN
Baptiste	Baptist	BA
Juif	Jew	JU
Méthodistes wes-leyens britanniques	British Wesleyan Methodists	BWM
Méthodistes wes-leyens canadiens	Canadian Wesleyan Methodists	WM
Méthodistes épisco-paux	Episcopal Methodists	EM
Anabaptiste	Anabaptist	
Luthérien	Lutheran	LU
Quakers	Quakers	QU
Tunkers	Tunkers	TU
Moraviens	Moravians	MO or MV
l'Église réformée de la Hollande	Dutch reformed church	

Figure 38-1: Religious denominations

39
Terms and Phrases Found in Baptism Records

In previous chapters, we looked at some of the more common terms and phrases found in church records. These included numbers, dates, abbreviations, and relationship terms. The priests from any given location and time period followed a format as they entered the record into the registers. This boilerplate text helps even a French language neophyte to, at the very least, pick out crucial information from the record.

But as we all know, some records contain unusual terms. Some do not follow the pattern. Then what?

In this chapter, we will review the common terms as well as add some of the more uncommon terms to our list.

Another consideration is that the further back in time you go, the more difficult it is to read the handwriting. In Appendix B, I've provided a Handwriting Chart that you can use for any document with difficult writing. It lists the alphabet by capital and lowercase letters. Look for words that you are positive about and copy the known letters into the chart exactly the way the scribe wrote them. It will then be easier to decipher the words you have trouble with. This is especially useful for capital letters.

As we learned in chapter 34, the date usually appears first in a baptism record. The priest may start by writing *le dix-huit septembre,* or "the 18th of September," followed by the year. Or he may substitute *ce* meaning "this" instead of *le* meaning "the," so it reads "this 18th of September." *Aujourd'hui le dix-huit septembre* means "today, the 18th of September," followed by the year. Sometimes the priest would start with the year rather than the date, such as *l'an mil sept cent treize,* or "the year (*l'an*) 1713," followed by the date, *le dix-huit septembre.* The priest could use *cejourd'hui* in place of *aujourd'hui,* which means "this day" or "today" (Figure 39-1).

Date Variations	
le dix huit septembre	the 18th of September
ce dix huit septembre	this 18th of September
aujourd'hui le dix-huit septembre	today the 18th of September
l'an mil sept cent treize le dix huit septembre	the year 1713 the 18th of September
cejourd'hui	this day, today

Figure 39-1: Date variations in baptism records

Next come the words the priest uses to refer to himself as the person recording the information. A very common method is *par nous prêtre curé soussigné,* with or without the word *curé,* which means "by we the undersigned priest." (The priest is using the "royal we.")(Figure 39-2)

You may also see *nous prêtre vicaire soussigné,* a *vicaire* being the curate or assistant to the parish priest. For the differences between *prêtre, curé,* and *vicaire,* the late Father John Sullivan, known as Owentagart on the Québec-research list, responded to this topic in a reply that he gave back on April 22, 2001.

Priest	
par nous prêtre curé soussigné a été baptisé[e]	by we the undersigned priest was baptized
nous prêtre curé soussigné avons baptisé	we the undersigned parish priest have baptized
je prêtre soussigné ai baptisé	I the undersigned priest have baptized

Figure 39-2: Priest references in baptism records

One of the difficulties here is that the cognate words have differing references in English and in French. Another is that there are differences between "Roman Catholic" and "Anglican" usages of the English words. And there are differences between "Canadian" and "USA" usages, as well.

He goes on to explain the Catholic usage.

"Prêtre" is precisely translated as "priest." It refers to a man who has received the sacrament of Holy Orders in the order of presbyter.

"Curé" is translated "parish priest" in British/Canadian usage, and "pastor" in US usage. It refers to a priest who has pastoral responsibility for a parish. But the Anglican translation of "curé" is "vicar."

"Vicaire" is usually translated "curate" when it refers to the assistant priest in a parish. In some places south of the border, the current term is "parochial vicar." "Vicaire" and "vicar" are also found in such expressions as "grand vicaire" or "vicaire général" (translated Vicar General), the highest ranking executive officer of a diocese other than the bishop), and "vicaire judiciaire" (translated Judicial Vicar), the chief judicial officer of the diocese, and chief judge of the Tribunal.

Although most priests seemed to use the "royal we," occasionally you will find a priest who was grammatically correct. He would write, *Je prêtre soussigné*, or "I, the undersigned priest." This priest would then continue with the words, *ai baptisé* for "I have baptized." The priests who referred to themselves as the royal we (*nous*) use *avons baptisé*, maintaining plural consistency. The difference is to make sure that the verb agrees with the subject of the sentence, "I" or "we."

Now we're going to expand and go a bit more in depth on the gender clues we discussed in chapter 28. There we learned that when *baptisé* ended in an *e-accent aigu*, the baptized subject was male. If *baptisée* ended in an *e-accent aigu -e*, then the subject was female. This did not apply if the priest simply said *je prêtre soussigné ai baptisé* or *nous prêtre soussigné avons baptisée*. Here the priest is saying either "I" or "we" the undersigned priest have baptized . . . ." In that case, "baptized" is part of a verb phrase and does not have to agree with the gender of the person who was baptized.

Sometimes a priest begins this section of the record with the word *par* for "by." It continues with "by we, the undersigned priest" followed by the words *a été baptisé*, or "was baptized." Then comes the name of the subject. "By we, the undersigned priest, was baptized Jean-Baptiste," for example. Since *été* is from the verb "to be" (*étre*), then *baptisé* (*baptisée* for females) *does* need to agree with the subject of the baptism, whether male or female.

Next you will see, only if applicable, the words *sous condition* which means that the priest baptized the child conditionally. This occurred when someone at home, usually the *sage-femme* (midwife) or the father, already baptized the child because of concerns that the child was weak or ill and may not survive long enough to make it to a priest. If there were such concerns and the baby *was* baptized by someone present at the birth, then the child was baptized *ondoyé* (for a boy) and *ondoyée* (for a girl).

There are a few other terms you may occasionally come across in reference to twins. If the twins were both boys or a boy and a girl, you will see the word *jumeaux*. If both babies are girls, they are *jumelles*. If the child was illegitimate, you will sometimes, but not always, see the word *naturel* (Figure 39-3).

Children	
jumeaux	twin boys, or one boy and one girl
jumelles	twin girls
naturel	illegitimate

Figure 39-3: Children references in baptism records

Next comes the name of the child minus the surname. The surname is usually given in the margin and as part of the father's complete name. If you're having trouble deciphering the given names, you can find hints and suggestions in chapter 2, Given Names and Diminutives.

The priest then tells us when the child was born following the word *né* for boys and *née* for girls. Common phrases are *aujourd'hui* or *le même jour* (literally "the same day") for "today," *hier* for "yesterday" or "the day before," *la veille* for "the evening before," *avant hier* for "the day before yesterday," and *avant veille* or *surveille* for "two days ago" (Figure 39-4).

Day of birth (follows *né* or *née*)	
aujourd'hui	today
le même jour	the same day
hier	yesterday
la veille	the evening before
avant hier	the day before yesterday
avant veille	two days ago
surveille	two days ago
le neuf du courant mois	the ninth of the current month
depuis trois jours	since three days, or three days ago
ce jour	this day

Figure 39-4: Day of birth references in baptism records

Although most children were baptized the same day or within a day or two of birth, there were also times when an immediate baptism was not possible. You might see *née le dix du courant* (born the tenth of the current month). If this appeared in a record where the child was baptized the 22nd of March, then she was born on the 10th of March. In another record, it is stated slightly differently. It reads, *"née le neuf du courant mois,"* or "born the ninth of the current month."

You will discover instances when the baptism did not take place until months or occasionally even years after the birth. An example is when a family lived in a remote area serviced by traveling priests. Then you might see several children of different ages from the same family all baptized on the same day.

If you see something like *né depuis trois jours*, where *trois* can be any number, it means the child was "born since three days" or "three days ago." *Né ce jour* means "born this day."

Next the priest will tell you that the child was born "from the legitimate marriage of," or *du légitime mariage de*. Occasionally this will read differently. After the day of birth, you might see *fils* or *fille légitime de*, indicating that the child is the legitimate son or daughter of. This also verifies that the marriage was legitimate. Sometimes the words were reversed. Instead of *du légitime mariage de*, the priest might write *du mariage légitime de*. This means the same thing (Figure 39-5).

Marriage information	
du légitime marriage de	of the legitimate marriage of (followed by the father's name and occupation)
fils légitime de	legitimate son of
fille légitime de	legitimate daughter of
du mariage légitime de	from the legitimate marriage of

Figure 39-5: Marriage references in baptism records

Following this are the names and residence of the parents. If the father's name begins with a vowel, the previous *de* will be *d'*, as in *du légitime mariage d'Antoine* (of the legitimate marriage of An-

toine). You will find the father's complete name, including surname and *dit* name if he had one, usually followed by his occupation (Figure 39-6). The two most commonly seen occupations are *cultivateur* (husbandman or farmer) and *journalier* (day la-

Common occupations	
cultivateur	cultivator (farmer) or husbandman
journalier	day laborer
meunier	miller
forgeron	blacksmith

Figure 39-6: Occupation references in baptism records

borer). You might also find in your family a *meunier* (miller) or a *forgeron* (blacksmith). See Appendix I for an extensive list of French occupations and their English translations.

Next comes the name of the mother. If you're having a difficult time deciphering her surname, check for a similar name in the mention of the godparents at the end of the record. Check signatures. If the mother signed, perhaps her signature is more legible. If a member of the mother's family was a godparent, maybe that surname is easier to read (Figure 39-7).

Mother	
et de (d')	and of (followed by name of mother)

Figure 39-7: Reference to the mother in baptism records

Places	
du lieu	of this place
de cette paroisse	of this parish
de or du [name of parish]	of [name of parish]
du susdit township	of the aforesaid township

Figure 39-8: Place references in baptism records

In the majority of cases, the parents were *de cette pariosse*, "of this parish," or the parish in which the priest performed the baptism. The priest might use the phrase *du lieu* for "of this place." In one instance, the priest baptized the child *dans le township d'Upton*, or "in the township of Upton." When stating the residence of the parents, he indicated *du susdit township*, "of the aforesaid township" (Figure 39-8).

For the godparents, you may see the word *parrain* for "godfather" followed by his name and the word *marrain* for "godmother" followed by her name. Sometimes the priest wrote a more complete sentence: *Le parrain a été* [name of godfather] *et la marrain* [name of godmother] for "The godfather was (name) and the godmother..." If the godparents are a married couple, the priest will sometimes indicate that by writing *son épouse* (his wife) after the name of the godmother. You might instead see *femme de* (wife of) and the husband's name. If the godmother is a widow, the priest may indicate that and include the name of the deceased husband (*veuve de...*). Those are the gems you *hope* to find (Figure 39-9).

The last sentence can provide interesting information. It tells you whether or not the godparents and the father of the child could sign their names, and whether or not the father was present for the baptism (Figure 39-10). If either of the godpar-

Godparents	
parrain	godfather
marrain	godmother
le parrain a été	The godfather was
le marrain a été	The godmother was
son épouse	his wife
femme de	wife of
veuve de	widow of

Figure 39-9: References to godparents in baptism records

ents could sign his or her name, and the signatures are of a different handwriting than the remainder of the record, then you have an actual signature, not one copied by the scribe to submit the civil copy. The mother was rarely present for the baptism. If the father was not present, there could be several reasons. He could be in the military; he could be a *voyageur* (fur trader); he could be away on business; he could be in jail. There are a multitude of reasons, and it's a lucky genealogist who can find a substantiating document of explanation.

Signatures	
n'ont su signé	have not signed
qui n'ont su signer, le père était absent	who could not sign, the father was absent

Figure 39-10: Signature references in baptism records

Occasionally in the middle of the record, you will find a raised hashtag or number sign. That means that the priest accidentally left out one or more words from that spot. If you look in the margin, you will find the hashtag and the missing words initialed by the priest.

If French is not your native language, I would suggest that you make a copy of your baptism record because you'll be marking it up quite a bit. Take a highlighter, look through this chapter, and highlight the words and phrases that we've covered and that are more common. Then take out the phrases in between and deal with them one by one. If you need to, have someone translate them. Keep track of these words or phrases on the My Baptism Terms/Phrases chart (Appendix B) in case you run into them again.

Where to Find French-Canadian Baptism Records

You can find original baptism records on Drouin microfilms located at various repositories. You will find them online in several places, including on Familysearch.org in their free collection titled *Quebec Catholic Parish Registers, 1621–1979*.[40] Take some time to read the collection description.[41] Scroll down and read *Known Issues with This Collection* before you begin your search.

Another terrific source for these images is the LaFrance collection.[42] This is a paid site that, in my opinion, is well worth the money. Your search produces an index card with a link in the upper right corner to the actual image. It can't get much easier than that. Be sure to check the current date range as they are continually adding more records.

You'll also find these parish records in Ancestry's *Quebec, Canada, Vital and Church Records (Drouin Collection), 1621–1968*.[43] There is a subscription fee for home use. Some libraries provide access for their patrons.

---

[40] https://www.familysearch.org/search/collection/1321742

[41] https://familysearch.org/wiki/en/Quebec,_Catholic_Parish_Registers_(FamilySearch_Historical_Records)#Known_Issues_with_This_Collection

[42] https://www.genealogiequebec.com

[43] https://search.ancestry.com/search/db.aspx?dbid=1091

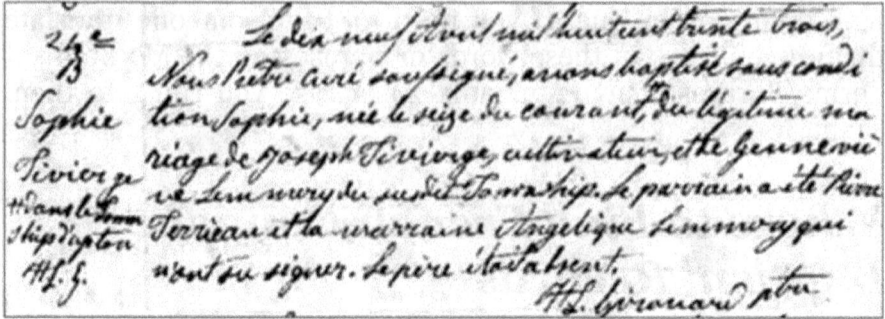

Figure 39-11: Baptism sample document

Sample Document

Transcription

<u>Margin</u> (Figure 39-11)

a: 24e
b: B
c: Sophie
d: Tivierge
e : #dans le Town
f : ship d'Upton
g : #L. G.

<u>Record</u>

1: Le dix-neuf Avril mil huit cent trente trois,
2 : Nous Prêtre Curé soussigné, avons baptisé sous condi
3 : tion Sophie, née le seize du courant, # du légitime ma
4 : riage de Joseph Tivierge, cultivateur, et de Genneviè
5 : ve Lemmery du susdit Township. Le parrain a été Pierre
6 : Terrieau et la marraine Angelique Lemmery qui
7 : n'ont su signer. Le père était absent.
8 :   HL [?] Girouard ptre

Translation

<u>Margin</u>

a: This was the 24th (vingt-quatrième) baptism recorded that year.
b: B=baptism
c: child's given name
d: child's surname
e: In the record, the priest accidentally omitted the child's birthplace. He inserted a hashtag, then wrote a corresponding hashtag in the margin with the missing information. #in the Town-[priests often omitted hyphens]
f: rest of the word "Township;" Township of Upton
g: another hashtag with the priest's initials

<u>Record</u>

1: The 19th of April 1833
2: We the undersigned priest curè have baptised under condition (The child was brought to the priest three days after birth. Someone had conditionally baptised the child in case she died before making it to a priest.)
3: rest of the word "condition"; Sophie, born the 16th of the current month, # (leading to "in the Township of Upton" in the margin), of the legitimate marriage
4: rest of the word *mariage*; of Joseph Tivierge, farmer, and of Geneviève
5: rest of the name Geneviève; Lemmery of the aforesaid Township. The godfather was Pierre
6: Terrieau and the godmother Angelique Lemmery who
7: did not sign. The father was absent.
8:                 HL Girouard, priest

40
Terms and Phrases Found in Marriage Records

When the parish priest recorded a marriage, he followed a particular format as he did with baptism and burial records. This format could vary slightly due to time period or location, but, for the most part, the records were very similar. However, marriage records exhibit the greatest degree of variation due to their greater length and complexity.

The information included in most marriage records is the names, residences, and parents of the bride and groom. The record notes whether or not the bride and groom reached the age of majority. We discover in which parish the parents resided, who the witnesses were, and occasionally how the witnesses were related to the bride or groom. Sometimes we learn the occupations of males mentioned in the document. Many 17th- century records also give the origins in France for the bride, the groom, or their parents if they were immigrants.

A genealogist considers himself very fortunate to discover a marriage record filled with much more than the basics. But how frustrating it is if you can't read it! This additional information could hold just the clue you need to break through a brick wall or distinguish two people with the same name. But it is such a tease to see phrases or sentences interspersed throughout the document when you don't have the key to unlock their meanings. So let's rectify that!

French-Canadian marriage records usually begin with the date. If you need a refresher, see chapter 32, *French Numbers*; chapter 33, *Ordinal Numbers*; and chapter 34, *French Dates*.

After the date you will normally see the words *après la publication de trois bans de mariage faites aux prônes de nos messes paroissiales*, or "after the publication of three banns of marriage[44] made during the sermon of our parish mass." Sometimes you will see the word *consecutif*, meaning that the three banns were announced during consecutive masses. This was the normal procedure.[45]

If something unusual occurred, if for some reason one, two, or all three banns were eliminated, there would be a mention of that in the marriage record. You will usually find it near the beginning of the record, with mention of the impediments (*les empêchements*) [46] and the dispensation (*dispense*) [47] appearing either

---

[44] Banns of marriage were notices of an impending marriage usually given during three consecutive parish masses.

[45] For more details on banns of marriage, listen to Maple Stars and Stripes episode #15, *French-Canadian Marriage Records* at http://maplestarsandstripes.com/15.

[46] An impediment is a hindrance to a lawful marriage. An impediment might occur due to the age of the bride or groom or because of a close relationship of consanguinity or affinity. Consanguinity indicates a relationship through blood by descent from a common ancestor. Affinity is a relationship due to marriage.

[47] A dispensation is the relaxation of a church law granted by an appropriate church official.

directly after the impediment or toward the end before mention of the witnesses.

In a marriage record for François Parent and Arméline Piquette, they received a dispensation because the marriage was taking place on March 11th, during Lent. Easter that year was on April 1st. The dispensation was granted by the archbishop of Montreal both for the date and for a second degree of collateral consanguinity. This information all appears at the beginning of this document (Figure 40-1).

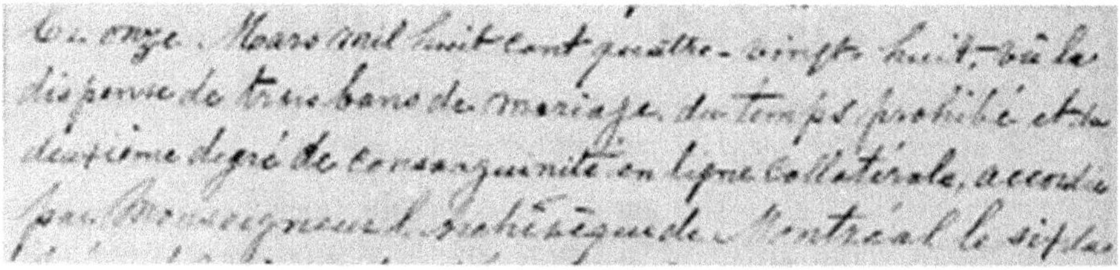
Le onze Mars mil huit cent quatre-vingt-huit, vu la
dispense de trois bans de mariage, du temps prohibé et du
deuxième degré de consanguinité en ligne collatérale, accordée
par Monseigneur l'Archevêque de Montréal le soussi

Figure 40-1: Marriage record with dispensation

However, in the marriage record of Moise Girard and Virginie Bastien, we learn after the date that only two banns were published without opposition (Figure 40-2). We need to look further down the document, after the information regarding the bride, the groom, and their parents, to find out that the dispensation was sanctioned by the Monseigneur of Trois-Rivières (Figure 40-3).

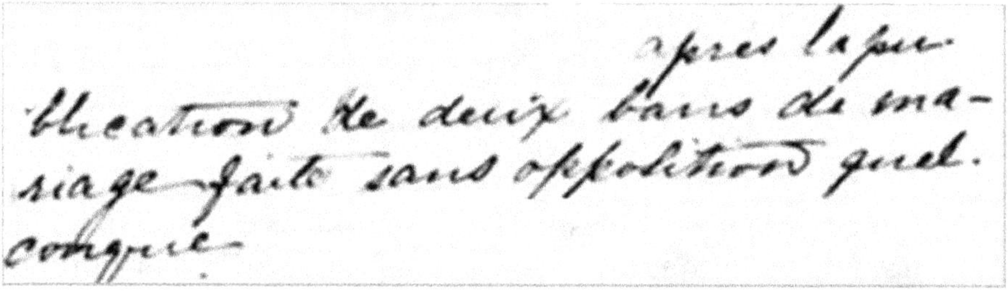
après la pu-
blication de deux bans de mariage faite sans opposition quel-
conque

Figure 40-2: Marriage record with two banns published without opposition

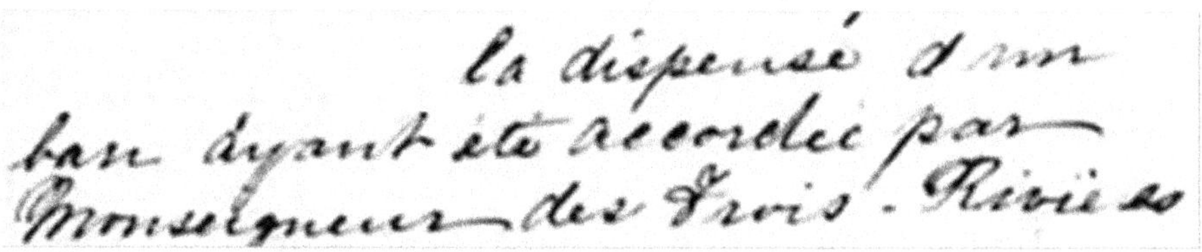
la dispense d'un
ban ayant été accordée par
Monseigneur des Trois-Rivières

Figure 40-3: Marriage record with dispensation by the Monseigneur of Trois-Rivières

In the marriage record of René Pelletier and Marie Magdelaine Leclerc in 1691, the priest is very specific. The banns were read on the day of the Feast of Saints Simon and Jude, the day of the Feast of All the Saints, and the following Sunday. That would be October 28th, November 1, and November 4th, three consecutive required days of church attendance (Figure 40-4).

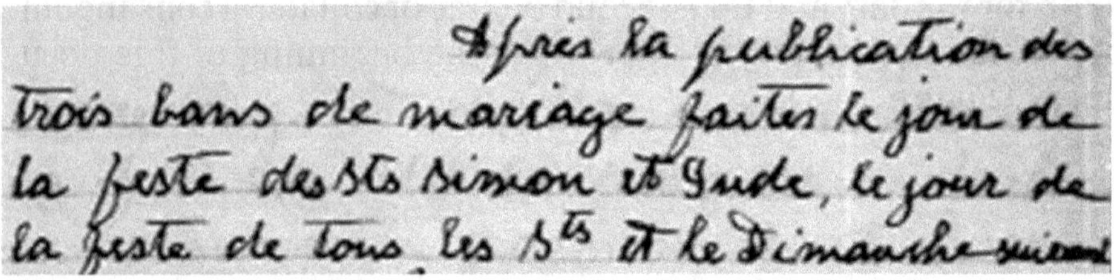
Après la publication des trois bans de mariage faites le jour de la feste des Sts Simon et Jude, le jour de la feste de Tous les Sts et le Dimanche suivant

Figure 40-4: Marriage record with dates that banns were read

Marriage records give the groom's information followed by that of the bride. That information will usually include name, residence, whether he or she has reached the age of majority, occupation for men, parents' names, parents' residences, and a possible notation indicating that one or both parents are deceased. If it is not the first marriage for either the bride or groom, it will say that he or she is widowed followed by the name of the deceased spouse.

Let's go over each section in detail, beginning with the groom's information (For terms, see Figure 40-5).

The groom's name is usually followed by *fils de* (son of), *fils mineur de* (minor son of), or *fils majeur de*, meaning the groom has reached the age of majority. Next you might see his occupation (see Appendix I for a list of occupations in French and the English translations) and whether or not he resided in the parish of record or another named parish. The parish of record was usually the parish of the bride. If the bride, the groom, or either of their parents resided in that same parish, you will see the French words *de cette paroisse* (of this parish). If either of them resided in a different parish, you might see the words *de la paroisse de...* (of the parish of...) followed by the name of the parish, including 17th-century French parishes. Following the groom's parish are the names of his parents, an indication if they were deceased (*feu/feue* or *défunt/défunte*), and the parents' residence. This will be followed by the words *d'une part* indicating that they are one party involved in this agreement.

The bride's information follows that of the groom. She will either be the *fille de* (daughter of), *fille mineure de* (minor daughter of), or *fille majeure de*, meaning she was of age. (Remember that when you add a final *e* to a noun or adjective, that word changes from masculine to feminine. See chapter 25 for a refresher.) If you don't know a date of birth, then pay attention to whether or not the bride or groom had reached the age of majority. This can be helpful to narrow down a date range when looking for a baptism record or trying to separate two people with the same name.

Next comes the phrase telling us that the bride makes up the second party involved in the record, *d'autre part*, or "the other party."

If it was not the first marriage for either the bride or groom, the record will not name their parents, but rather their previous spouse. Since divorce was rare to nonexistent, you will usually see the

Terms and Phrases Found in French-Canadian Marriage Records	
French	**English**
de cette paroisse	of this parish
de la paroisse de…	of the parish of…
fils de	son of
fils mineur de	minor son of
fils majeur de	son (who has reached age of majority) of
fille de	daughter of
fille mineure de	minor daughter of
fille majeure de	daughter (who has reached age of majority) of
veuf de	widower of
veuve de	widow of
veuf majeur	widower who has reached the age of majority
feu	deceased (m)
défunt	deceased (m)
feue	deceased (f)
défunte	deceased (f)
des feux	of the deceased (plural)
veuve de feu…	widow of the late…
l'époux	the husband
l'épouse	the wife
de plusieurs autres	of several others

Figure 40-5: French words found in marriage records

words *veuf de* for "widower of" or *veuve de* for "widow of." To find the parents, you should go back and find the previous marriage.

Once you're familiar with these words, it becomes easier to understand the rare combinations you may come across. For example, in the marriage of François Parent to Arméline Piquette, François is listed as the *veuf majeur* de Marguerite Lausson. *Veuf majeur* means he was the widower of Marguerite Lausson, but he had reached the age of majority.

Two other important words are those that indicate that a person had died. You will see either *feu* or *défunt* for a deceased male and *feue* or *défunte* for a deceased female. This information is found in two different locations: either describing the parents of either the bride or groom, or describing a previous spouse.

In the marriage between François Paquet and Angélique Paradis, François was the son of *feu* Guillaume Paquet, or the son of the "deceased" Guillaume Paquet. Angélique was the daughter of *des feux* Pierre Paradis and Marie Miloy. In *des feux*, both words are the plural forms of the words "of" and "deceased," indicating that she had already lost both parents. In Marie Philomine Forest's marriage, she was the daughter of the *défunte* Justine Forest, indicating her mother had died.

In the Parent/Piquette marriage, it is emphasized that she is the *veuve de feu* Joseph Brault, or the "widow of the deceased" Joseph Brault.

After the names of the groom, the fathers of the bride and groom, and occasionally the male witnesses, you will find an occupation, such as *cultivateur* (cultivator/farmer), which is very common. For a list of French occupations and their English translations, see Appendix I.

Either at the top after the date or at the bottom before the witnesses, you will occasionally see mention of dispensations. If there were none, then at the bottom of the record before the witness information you might see words telling you that there were no impediments to the marriage. The consent of the parents was received if an underage bride or groom was involved. Then the priest gave the nuptial blessing in the presence of the witnesses. (Example: *ne s'étant découvert aucun empéchement au dit mariage et de l'avis des parens nous prêtre soussigné avons reçu leur mutuel consentement et leur avons donné la bénédiction nuptiale en présence de* [witnesses]). If the bride and groom were of age, then the priest received the mutual consent of the bride and groom (*reçu leur mutuel consentement*).

After the priest recorded that he had married the couple, he then listed the witnesses. Those related to the groom appear first, sometimes with their exact relationship to *l'époux* (the husband). Then come the witnesses for *l'épouse* (the wife). Male relations might be *père* (father) or *frère* (brother), two of the most common. You also might see *oncle* (uncle), *cousin* (cousin), *beau-frère* (brother-in-law), *grand-père* (grandfather), or *ami* (friend). For female witnesses, although rarer, you could find *mère* (mother), *soeur* (sister), *tante* (aunt), *cousine* (cousin), *belle-soeur* (sister-in-law), *grand-mère* (grandmother), and *amie* (a female friend). The priest might end with *de plusieurs autres*, or "of several others," to encompass any other guests present (Figure 40-6).

The priest then indicated whether any among those present were able to sign the document. It's a great day when your ancestor could write, and you are now blessed with a copy of his or her actual signature!

That is the gist of a marriage record. But as I said before, out of the three vital records, this is

Familial Relationships	
French	**English**
Père	Father
Frére	Brother
Oncle	Uncle
Cousin	Cousin (m)
Beau-frère	Brother-in-law
Grand-père	Grandfather
Ami	Friend (m)
Mére	Mother
Soeur	Sister
Tante	Aunt
Cousine	Cousin (f)
Belle-soeur	Sister-in-law
Grand-mère	Grandmother
Amie	Friend (f)

Figure 40-6: Familial relationships

the one that has the greatest degree of variation from record to record.

For example, in the marriage record of Jean Collet and Jeanne Dechard, after the date and the name of the groom, there's information telling us that the groom was a soldier in the company of Messieur Petit in the Carignan-Salière Regiment. If you don't read French very well, those rare words might confuse you. With practice you can pick out the important information, but sometimes it's that one phrase that you can't read that hides valuable information.

If French is not your native language, I would suggest that you make a copy of your marriage record (make sure it's a copy of your original because you'll be marking it up quite a bit). Take a highlighter, look through this chapter, and highlight the words and phrases that we've covered and that are more common. Then take out the phrases in between and deal with them one by one. If needed, have someone translate them. Keep track of these words or phrases on the My Marriage Terms/Phrases chart (Appendix B) in case you run into them again.

The French words in these documents will become more and more familiar over time and with lots of practice.

Where to Find French-Canadian Marriage Records

Where do you go to find original French-Canadian marriage records? Of course, you can find them in the original parishes in Québec. Assuming it's too far to travel, there are physical repositories as well as online sites that might be a bit more convenient. Many genealogy libraries or large research libraries carry the Drouin microfilms of either the original records or the civil copy located in the archives.

Online you can find the digital images at familysearch.org. This is a free collection titled *Quebec Catholic Parish Registers, 1621–*

1979.[48] Take some time to read the collection description.[49] Be sure to scroll down and read *Known Issues with This Collection* before you begin your search.

Another terrific source for these images is the LaFrance collection.[50] This is a paid site that, in my opinion, is well worth the money. Your search produces an index card with a link in the upper right corner to the actual image. It can't get much easier than that.

You'll also find these parish records in Ancestry's *Quebec, Canada, Vital and Church Records (Drouin Collection), 1621–1968.*[51] There is a subscription fee for home use. Some libraries provide access for their patrons.

Sample Document

Transcription

Margin (Figure 40-7)

a: M13
b : Js Parent
c : +
d : Amanda Forgues

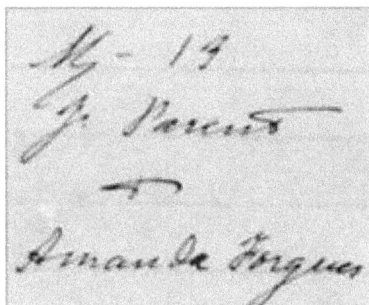

Figure 40-7: Marriage sample margin

Record (Figure 40-8)

1 : Le trois Novembre mil huit cent quatre vingt
2 : dix-sept, après la publication de trois bans de
3 : mariage faite au prône de notre messe
4 : paroissiale, entre Joseph Parent fils mi-
5 : neur de Prospère Parent, cultivateur, et
6 : de défunte Olivine Lévéque, de cette paroisse

---

[48] https://www.familysearch.org/search/collection/1321742
[49] https://familysearch.org/wiki/en/Quebec,_Catholic_Parish_Registers_(FamilySearch_Historical_Records)#Known_Issues_with_This_Collection
[50] https://www.genealogiequebec.com
[51] https://search.ancestry.com/search/db.aspx?dbid=1091

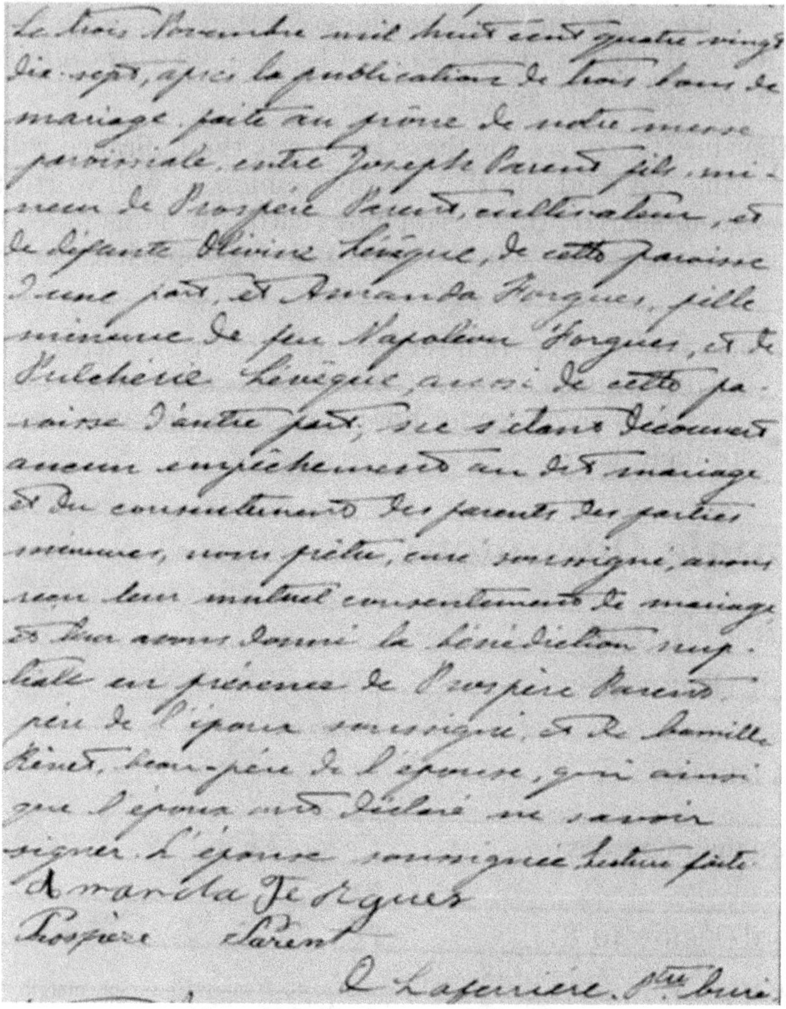

Figure 40-8 : Marriage sample document

7 : d'une part, et Amanda Forgues, fille
8 : mineure de feu Napoléon Forgues, et de
9 : Pulchérie Lévéque, aussi de cette pa-
10 : roisse d'autre part; ne s'étant découvert
11 : aucun empêchement au dit mariage
12 : et du consentement des parents des parties
13 : mineures, nous prêtre, curé soussigné, avons
14 : reçu leur mutuel consentement de mariage,
15 : et leur avons donné la bénédiction nup-
16 : tiale en présence de Prospère Parent,
17 : père de l'époux soussigné, et de Camille

18 : Rivet, beau-père de l'épouse, qui ainsi
19 : que l'époux ont déclaré ne savoir
20 : signer. L'épouse soussigné. Lecture faite.
Amanda Forgues
Prospère Parent

O Laferrière, P^{tre} Curé

Translation

Margin

a : This is the 13th marriage record for the year.
b: The groom is Js [Joseph] Parent
c: +=and
d: The bride is Amanda Forgues.

Record

1: The third of November 1880
2: 17 [The seventeen added to the 1880 from the previous line gives a year of 1897.]; after the publication of three bans of
3: marriage made during the sermon of our [parish] mass
4: The adjective for "parish" is the first word on this line; between Joseph Parent minor son [the word for "minor is split between both lines]
5: of Prosper Parent, farmer, and
6: of the late Olivine Lévéque, of this parish
7: of one party; and Amanda Forgues, [minor] daughter
8: minor of the late Napoléon Forgues, and of
9: Pulchérie Lévéque, also of this parish
10: Rest of the word "parish," of the other party; not having discovered
11: any impediment to the said marriage
12: and the consent of the parents of the [minor] parties
13: minor, we the priest, the undersigned curé, have
14: received their mutuel marriage consent
15: and have given them the nuptial blessing
16: Rest of the word "nuptial," in the presence of Prospère Parent,
17: father of the groom undersigned. and of Camille
18: Rivet, brother-in-law (or stepbrother) of the bride, who along
19: with the groom stated that they didn't know how
20: to sign. The undersigned bride. Reading made.

Amanda Forgues
Prospère Parent

O Laferrière, priest Curé

41
Terms and Phrases Found in Burial Records

The basic parts of a burial record are:

- ❖ Date
- ❖ Name of the deceased
- ❖ Occupation, if an adult
- ❖ Relationship to parents or spouse
- ❖ Day of death and age
- ❖ Names of witnesses
- ❖ Signatures

Burial records are the easiest of the three record types to decipher. Knowledge of a few key words and phrases will make it so much easier even if you can't read French well.

Priests wrote the name of each subject of the burial record in the margin for quick reference. He also wrote either an *S* for "burial" (*sépulture* in French) or a cross, as seen in the sample document at the end of the chapter (Figure 41-2).

All burial records begin with the date. Refer back to chapters 32–34 to become familiar with numbers and dates.

For a burial, you will usually find the phrase *a été inhumé* for "was buried." *Inhumé* indicates the deceased is a male. Add an *e* to the end for a female (*inhumée*). Priests also used the "royal we," as in *nous avons inhumé*, or "we have buried." In this case, *inhumé* will not match the gender of the deceased because *inhumé* is part of a verb phrase.

Dans le cemetière means "in the cemetery." *De cette paroisse* (of this parish) indicates the location of the burial. The priest is burying *le corps de* (the body of) followed by the name of the deceased. After an adult male's name, you will often see his occupation. For a list of French occupations and their English translations, see Appendix I.

Decedé and *mort* mean "died." Then come the "when" words. When did the deceased die?

If he died *hier*, he died yesterday. *La veille* or *le jour précedent* means he died the day before. *Avant hier* means "the day before yesterday."

Agé (with an added *e* for females) indicates the age at death. Following the number will either be the word *jour/jours* for "day/days"; *mois* for "month(s)"; or *ans* for "years." If a precise age is not known, you might see the word *environ* for "about" or "approximately."

If the deceased is a child, the record will state that he or she is the *fils* or *fille de* (son or daughter of) followed by the name of the parents. If the deceased is an adult, you might see *époux de* (husband of) or *épouse de* (wife of) followed by the spouse's name.

Présens for "present" is followed by the witnesses to the burial.

These words and phrases should cover most of the burial records you encounter.

Burial Terms	
a été inhumé(e)	was buried
Nous avons inhumé	we have buried
dans le cemetière	in the cemetery
de cette paroisse	of this parish
le corps	the body
decedé(e)	died
mort(e)	died
hier	yesterday
la veille	the night before
le jour précedent	the day before
avant hier	the day before yesterday
agé(e)	aged
jours	days
mois	months
ans	years
environ	about, approximately
fils de	son of
fille de	daughter of
époux de	husband of
épouse de	wife of
présens	present

Figure 41-1: Burial terms

If French is not your native language, I would suggest that you make a copy of the burial record (make sure it's a copy of your original because you'll be marking it up quite a bit). Take a highlighter, look through this chapter, and highlight the words and phrases that we've covered and that are more common. Then take out the phrases in between and deal with them one by one. If needed, have someone translate them. Keep track of these words or phrases on the *My Burial Terms/Phrases* chart (Appendix B) in case you run into them again.

The French words in these documents will become more and more familiar over time and with lots of practice.

Where to Find French-Canadian Burial Records

You can find original burial records on Drouin microfilms located at various repositories. You will find them online in several places, including on Familysearch.org in their free collection titled "*Quebec Catholic Parish Registers, 1621–1979.*[52] Take some

---

[52] https://www.familysearch.org/search/collection/1321742

time to read the collection description.[53] Be sure to scroll down and read *Known Issues with This Collection* before you begin your search.

Another terrific source for these images is the LaFrance collection.[54] This is a paid site that, in my opinion, is well worth the money. Your search produces an index card with a link in the upper right corner to the actual image. It can't get much easier than that.

You'll also find these parish records in Ancestry's *Quebec, Canada, Vital and Church Records (Drouin Collection), 1621–1968*.[55] There is a subscription fee for home use. Some libraries provide access for their patrons.

Sample Document

Transcription

Margin (Figure 41-2)
a: +
b: Marie Louise
c: Picard
d: dite
e : Destroismaisons

Record (Figure 41-3)

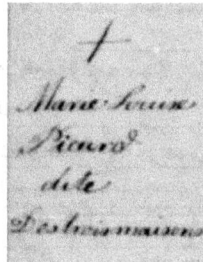

Figure 41-2 : Burial sample margin

1: Aujourdhui le quatre janvier mil huit cent trente quatre nous prêtre soussigne
2: avons inhumée dans le simétière [*sic*] de cette paroisse le corps de Marie Louise
3: décédée avant-hier; âgée de soixante cinq ans Epouse de Pierre Sourdif présens

---

[53]https://familysearch.org/wiki/en/Quebec,_Catholic_Parish_Registers_(FamilySearch_Historical_Records)#Known_Issues_with_This_Collection
[54] https://www.genealogiequebec.com
[55] https://search.ancestry.com/search/db.aspx?dbid=1091

4: Paul Sourdif et Pierre Sourdif tous deux enfants de la défunte que nont su
5: signer   Ls. O. Deligny p^{tre}

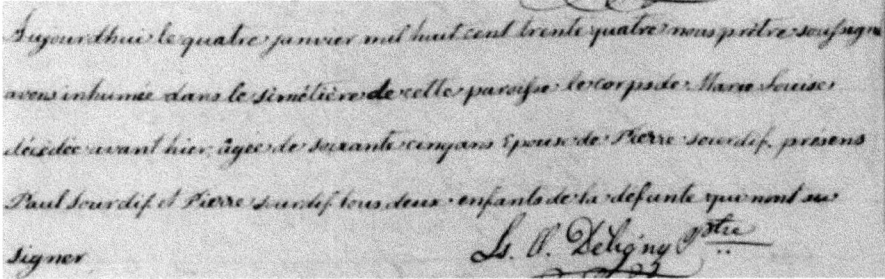

Figure 41-3: Burial sample document

Translation

<u>Margin</u>

a: For a burial, you'll see either the letter *S* or this cross symbol.
b: Marie Louise
c: Picard
d: The feminine form of *dit*, meaning "also known as" or "called."
e: Destroismaisons (the *dite* name)

<u>Record</u>

1: Today the fourth of January 1834 we the undersigned priest
2: have buried in the cemetery of this parish the body of Marie Louise
3: deceased the day before yesterday; sixty-five years old wife of Pierre Sourdif present
4: Paul Sourdif and Pierre Sourdif both children of the deceased who did not
5: sign   Ls. O. Deligny priest

42
Geographical Terms

For French-Canadian researchers new to the task, inevitable questions arise regarding place names. When did a particular place change its name? Is this place a parish or a town? Do I hyphenate the name or not? How should I record this place in my genealogy software program?

Time and Place

Let's start with a chronological look at naming practices for the largest regions of the area.

Nouvelle France

We see the use of the term **Nouvelle France**, "New France" in English, beginning with Jacques Cartier's exploration of the Gulf of Saint Lawrence in **1534**. At its greatest extent, this territory included lands from Newfoundland in the east to the western prairies and from Hudson Bay in the north to the Gulf of Mexico in the south. France's claim to these colonies ended in **1763** when they ceded New France to Great Britain.

Canada

When Jacques Cartier explored the territory in **1535**, the Natives called the area around present-day Quebec **kanata**. In **1547**, maps included the label **Canada** for all territory north of the St. Lawrence River. By **1616**, the regions around the St. Lawrence River and the Gulf of Saint Lawrence were called **Canada**. For several years, the lands from the St. Lawrence to the Gulf of Mexico were also known as **Québec**.

By the **early 1700s**, voyageurs and explorers had ventured into the territories to the west and south. As a result, **Canada** then referred to lands in the midwest as well as those along the Mississippi River to the Gulf of Mexico.

In **1791**, Canada became official as the province of Quebec was divided into **Upper Canada** (today's Ontario) and **Lower Canada** (today's Quebec).

Upper and Lower Canada were united in **1841** and became the **Province of Canada**, with Ontario also called **Canada West** and Quebec referred to as **Canada East**.

On **July 1, 1867**, the province of Canada was divided into **Ontario** and **Québec**. They along with Nova Scotia and New Brunswick became the **Dominion of Canada**.

Québec

Quebec City was founded by Samuel Champlain and others in **1608**. In the **17th and early 18th centuries**, the term **Québec** was loosely used for all the lands from the Saint Lawrence River to the Gulf of Mexico.

After the conquest, Britain's Royal Proclamation of **1763** created the **Province of Québec** which eventually extended from Labrador to the area between the Great Lakes and the Ohio and Mississippi Rivers.

Montréal

Originally called **Ville-Marie**, the area of present-day Old Montréal was settled in **1642**. Nearby was a volcanic mountain named *Mont-Réal* ("Royal Mountain" in English). **Montréal** became the name of the island, and **by 1705** it became the official name of the city, although the name had been used unofficially for a while.

Pays d'en Haut

From **1639 to 1763**, the vast territory north and west of Montréal, including all the lands that the French explored beyond the Great Lakes, was known as the ***pays d'en haut***, or "Upper Country."

Now it's just Canada!

| General Geopolitical Timeline ||
Name	Time period
Canada (New France)	1608 to 1763
Province of Québec	1763 to December 26, 1791
The Canadas (Lower Canada and Upper Canada)	December 26, 1791 to February 10, 1841
Province of Canada (Canada East and Canada West)	February 10, 1841 to July 1, 1867
Dominion of Canada	July 1, 1867 to after WWII

Figure 42-1: General geopolitical timeline

Parishes

Another question arises when genealogists are entering place names into their genealogy database program. What's a parish? What's a town? What's a county? Where are they located?

There are several different resources you can use. Keep in mind that not every village or *seigneurie* had a church. If your ancestor's village did not support a church, check the surrounding parishes.

Online

Map of Quebec's catholic parishes up to 1918[56] or *PRDH Map of Parishes*[57]

Villes présentes dans le Fichier Loiselle[58]

Quebec parishes's [*sic*] list sorted by name[59] and sorted by variant[60]

Books

Parish and Town Guide to the Province of Quebec published by Quintin Publications; has four sections listing parishes in chronological order and in alphabetical order by county, patron saint, and town: out of print; look for it in a library or at the FHL.

Reference & Guide Book for the Genealogist[61] published by the American-French Genealogical Society; also has a section listing Catholic churches of New England.

Guide to Quebec Catholic Parishes and Published Marriage Records by Jeanne Sauve White; lists parishes by diocese and then in chronological order by county; can also be found on Ancestry.com.

Dictionnaire historique et géographique des paroisses, missions et municipalités de la Province de Québec (Historical and Geographical Dictionary of Parishes . . .) by Hormisdas Magnan; text in French.

---

[56] https://www.genealogiequebec.com/en/LAFRANCE/map
[57] https://www.prdh-igd.com/en/Carte
[58] http://www.institutdrouin.com/loisellevilles.pdf
[59] http://www.genealogie.umontreal.ca/en/ListeParoissesSuivantNomUsuel
[60] http://www.genealogie.umontreal.ca/en/liste-des-paroisses-suivant-variante
[61] https://afgs.org/site/store/books-publications-other/

Hyphens

The last major question that arises is: Do I write the parish name with hyphens or not. For example, should I write St-François-de-Sales or St. François de Sales?

There are two schools of thought among genealogists. One is that you should always write a place name the way it appears in the original record, assuming you have access to that record. The other is that you should write it in a way most recognizable by your audience.

The definitive word comes from the Canadian Encyclopedia.[62] It says, "Hyphens are used in all populated place names of Québec with two or more words of French origin, thus Ste-Marthe-du-Cap-de-la-Madeleine, although names with initial articles do not have hyphens, for example, La Décharge, Le Grand-Village. Hyphens are not used in Québec names of non-French origin, for example, Campbell's Bay, Ayer's Cliff."

---

[62] http://www.thecanadianencyclopedia.ca/en/article/place-names/

Appendix

Appendix A:
Language Review

This section is a good place to begin reading this book. It gives an overview of the differences between the French and English languages. These differences will be explained in more detail in the individual chapters. Understanding these differences will help you make more sense of the records.

Germanic vs. Romance

Both English and French belong to the Indo-European language family. Think of it as the trunk of a tree. Germanic languages branched off in one direction. Romance languages with Latin as the root branched off in another direction. English is a Germanic language; French is a Romance language. For native English speakers, learning your first Romance language can be quite daunting. Yes, more than half of our English words come from Latin and French, both Romance languages. But what makes English Germanic is the underlying structure of the language itself.

Nouns

Let's start with nouns. In Romance languages, nouns have a gender attached to them. This includes words for inanimate objects not usually designated as male or female. French nouns are either masculine or feminine. Latin also has neuter nouns. Any adjective describing a noun has to agree with it in gender and number. So a French noun is either masculine singular, masculine plural, feminine singular, or feminine plural. The same goes for the French adjectives describing those nouns.

Here's an example. The noun "house" in English has four forms: house (singular), houses (plural), house's (singular possessive), and houses' (plural possessive). It is neither masculine nor feminine. To describe it as *big*, the form of the adjective does not change: the big house, the big houses, the big house's roof, the big houses' roofs.

In French, you first have to determine whether a noun is masculine or feminine. For words like "man" and "woman," it's easy. For a word like "house," not so much. You have to learn that the word for "house," *maison*, is a feminine noun. The adjective for "big" has to agree with "house" in gender (feminine) and number (singular or plural)—*grande maison* for the singular, *grandes maisons* for the plural.

The French word for "store," *magasin*, is masculine. To describe the store or the stores as big, you would use the adjectives *grand* and *grands*. One word, "big," in English becomes four words in French—*grande, grandes, grand,* and *grands*.

In French, adjectives also most often appear after the nouns they describe. In English, adjectives usually appear first. In English, we would say "the pretty girl"; in French they'd say "the girl pretty."

These concepts appear throughout this book. Understanding them will help you to translate and comprehend many details appearing in French genealogical records.

Verbs

The biggest adjustment for many Romance language novices is learning the verbs. We use a pronoun with our verbs to indicate who is doing the action. I like apples. You like apples. He likes apples. We like apples. They like apples. The pronoun tells us who is doing the action of liking the apples. The verb "like" stays the same, except for third person singular (he like**s**, she like**s**, it like**s**).

In Romance languages, the ending attached to the verb root tells us who is doing the action. We call this verb conjugation. In French, the same sentences are as follows: *J'aime les pommes. Tu aimes les pommes. Il aime les pommes. Nous aimons les pommes. Ils aiment les pommes.* In Latin, the preceding pronoun is not needed. Luckily, in French, the pronoun is usually present.

In English future tenses, we add the helping verb "will." In French, there is no helping verb. There is a future root form of the verb with endings clarifying the subject. "I will like" in French is *j'aimerai.* "He will like" is *il aimera.* "We will like" is *nous aimerons.*

Possessive

In English, we use an apostrophe plus *s* to denote the genitive case, or possessive. In Romance languages, you will see the word for "of" used instead. "The boy's kite" in English becomes "the kite of the boy" in a Romance language. For details on how this applies specifically to French, see chapter 27.

Diacriticals

Another difference between French and English is the use of diacriticals. These marks are not optional; they are part of the correct spelling of the word. For example, there's a difference in meaning between the French words *ou* and *où. Ou* means "or" in English; *où* means "where."

The three accent marks used in French words are the *accent aigu* (´), the *accent grave* (`) and the *accent circonflexe* (ˆ). They change the pronunciation of whichever letter they appear above. Other diacritical marks include the *cédille* (ç), which forces the sound of /s/ in front of certain letters. You will also see letters written with a *tréma* (¨), as in the name Noël. This indicates that both vowels are sounded.

Note: When writing this book, I decided to write the words "Quebec" and "Montreal" without the accent when writing in English and with the accent when using it in a French sentence or referring to a French record.

Phonics

Letters in French don't always make the same sounds in English, and vice versa; but knowing these sounds makes French-Canadian genealogy so much easier. If you know a surname in French, what did that name become after the family moved to America or another English-speaking territory? If you know the family's name in America and you're trying to trace them back to Quebec, what name should you be searching for in French records? Here is where phonics can help.

If you don't remember what *phonics* is, you're not alone. You probably haven't had a phonics lesson since elementary school. In the United States during the late 1940s and 1950s, some schools eliminated phonics from the curriculum. You may never have learned it.

So what is it? Phonics is a system that teaches people to decode words by sounds. After you learn individual sounds, you combine them to form words.

Since understanding French sounds is a large part of this book, I use various phonetic symbols to represent those sounds. Although I describe the symbols and sounds throughout the book, I wanted to put everything in one place for handy reference. Remember to use online apps like SitePal's *Text-to-Speech* [63]

---

[63] http://www.oddcast.com/home/demos/tts/tts_example.php

(mentioned in chapter 3). I like this one because it offers examples of Canadian French pronunciations.

Phonetic Symbols

Throughout this book, I use the same long and short vowel symbols we all learned in first grade phonics class. The symbols ā, ē, ī, ō, and ū represent the long vowel sounds, or the sound that matches the name of the letter. For short vowel sounds, you will see ă, ĕ, ĭ, ŏ, and ŭ. The symbol /ă/ is the vowel sound heard in /cat/; /ĕ/ is the vowel sound in /bed/; ĭ in /bit/; ŏ in /hot/; and ŭ in /cup/ (Figure A-1).

Most consonant sounds are the same in both French and English. However, there are a few sounds found in one but not the other. There are letters that make different sounds in each language. I cover these in depth in *Part 2, Understanding Pronunciation.*

I use italicized individual letters (*b*) to represent the written letter. A non-italicized letter inside slash marks (/b/) represents the *sound* of that letter. For example, take the sentence, "An *e* added to the end of a noun often changes that noun from masculine to feminine." The italicized *e* indicates a written *e*.

This long vowel symbol...	...makes the same sound as the vowel in this word.	This short vowel symbol...	...makes the same sound as the vowel in this word.
ā	lake	ă	cat
ē	sheet	ĕ	bed
ī	hike	ĭ	bit
ō	poke	ŏ	hot
ū	tune	ŭ	cup
ə (schwa)	syllable		

Figure A-1: Phonetic symbols

But in the sentence, "A *ch* in French sometimes makes the /sh/ sound," the *ch* represents the written letters. The /sh/ indicates the sound heard at the beginning of "shoe."

English also has multisyllabic words with an unstressed syllable. In the word "syllable," the middle syllable represented by the letter *a* is unstressed. We phonetically call this the schwa sound, /uh/. The symbol for this schwa sound is an upside down backward e, or ə. Any vowel (a, e, i, o, u, sometimes y) can make the schwa sound.

Hyphens are used to indicate the position of letters in a word. For example, *th*- tells us that the letters *th* appear at the beginning of a word followed by one or more other letters. On the other hand, *-tte* indicates that there are one or more letters followed by *tte*.

Nasal Sounds

There are several letter combinations in French pronounced with a nasal quality not heard in English speech. Misinterpretation of these sounds leads to many confusing and incorrect spellings in English. An example is the French surname Gamelin evolving into Gumlaw here in the States.

To better understand this, say the word "sung," but leave off the /s/ from the beginning of the word and the /g/ from the end of the word. The sound made by the letters *un* is one example of a nasal sound found in some French words. Another is the /an/ you hear in the word "hand" if you take away the initial /h/ and the final /d/.

Appendix B:
Charts, Forms, and
Worksheets

Handwriting Chart

Make several copies of the paleography guide (Figure B-1). Use one guide for each document or scribe.

When faced with a document that is difficult to read, look for recognizable words. Look for names, places, or months. Look for common words. When you are certain that you know a word, copy each individual capital and lower case letter into the guide, exactly the way the scribe wrote them.

When you come upon a word you don't know, check the guide. Look for recognizable letter shapes to determine the unknown word.

French Language Lifelines for the Anglo Genealogist

	Capital Letters		Capital Letters		Lower Case Letters		Lower Case Letters
A		P		a		p	
B		Q		b		q	
C		R		c		r	
D		S		d		s	
E		T		e		t	
F		U		f		u	
G		V		g		v	
H		W		h		w	
I		X		i		x	
J		Y		j		y	
K		Z		k		z	
L		É		l		é	
M		Î		m		è	
N				n		ê	
O				o		ç	
Document:							
Repository:							
Author/Scribe:							
Date:				Condition:			

Figure B-1: Handwriting chart

Other Resources

For several of the 17th and 18th-century notaries, check the 3-volume series *Initiation à la paléographie franco-canadienne: Les écritures des notaires aux XVIIe–XVIIIe siècles*[64] by Marcel Lafortune. The author analyzes the handwriting of each included notary. There are alphabet charts, samples of documents, samples of common words and phrases, and translations. Figure B-2 is a list of the notaries covered in each volume.

Volume 1	**Antoine Adhémar (1668–1714)**
	Bénigne Basset (1657–1699)
	Romain Becquet (1665–1682)
	Jean-Baptiste Daguilhe (1749–1783)
Volume 2	**Guillaume Audouart (1648–1663)**
	Cyr de Monmerqué (1730–1765)
	Daniel Normandin (1686–1729)
	Gilles Rageot (1666–1691)
Volume 3	**Guillaume Baret (1709–1744)**

Figure B-2: Notary handwriting samples found in *Initiation à la paléographie franco-canadienne*

The FamilySearch website has plenty of help for genealogists. *Language Resources and Handwriting Helps*[65] has handwriting guides as well as links to foreign language word lists. *French Handwriting*[66] includes tutorials for reading French records.

---

[64] Marcel Lafortune, *Initiation à la paléographie franco-canadienne: Les écritures des notaires aux XVIIe–XVIIIe siècles*, 3 vol. (Montréal: Société de recherche historique Archiv-Histo Inc., 1982–1988)

[65] https://www.familysearch.org/indexing/help/handwriting#!/lang=fr&title=Alphabet

[66] https://www.familysearch.org/wiki/en/French_Handwriting

My Baptism Terms/Phrases

Add your own baptism terms/phrases here.

French term	Translation

My Marriage Terms/Phrases

Add your own marriage terms/phrases here.

French term	Translation

My Burial Terms/Phrases

Add your own burial terms/phrases here.

French term	Translation

Step 1: Sounds Worksheet

See chapter 6, step 1 for instructions.

Search surname:	
Sounds in this surname:	
Sounds	**Letter combinations that make that sound**

Step 2: Surnames Worksheet

See chapter 6, step 2 for instructions.

Surname	Soundex	Surname	Soundex

Step 3: Soundex Worksheet

See chapter 6, step 3 for instructions.

Appendix C:
Answers
to Exercises

Chapter 4

Surname	Soundex
Tebo	T100
Thibeault	T143
Bauché	B200
Boscher	B260
Papineau	P150
Papinot	P153
Houde	H300
Oude	O300
Adhémar	A356
Cadieux	C320
Dallaire	D460

Chapter 33

the 24th day of July

Chapter 34

1) The 15th of November 1759
2) The 12th of August 1867
3) The 25th of June 1786

Appendix D: Navigating French Language Websites

For those who don't read French, navigating around French-language websites is an absolute chore. The first thing you should do is look to the top of the page for an *English* button. Even if you find one, often not all pages are translated. Depending on your browser, a *Translate* box may pop up when you fall on a French language page. Keep in mind that no mechanical translator is perfect. However, in most cases the narrative is good enough for you to get the general idea.

If you're on a page without an *English* button, and no *Translate* box pops up, copy and paste the website URL into a translation app like Google Translate.[67] This will work for narrative, but not databases.

---

[67] https://translate.google.com/

Common Website Navigation Terms	
accueil	welcome, home
à propos	about
contact	contact
nous joindre	contact
nous contacter	contact
nous écrire	contact
recherché, rechercher	search

Figure D-1: Common website navigation terms

If none of these is available, you may have to navigate on your own. Many people give up after a few minutes. With knowledge of a few key words, that chore can become a bit less tedious.

When you search for information, your inquiry sometimes takes you to a page buried deep in a website. The first thing you might want to do is navigate to the homepage. Look for the word *accueil*, which means "welcome" or "home." The About page is often indicated with the words *à propos*. There are several ways to write the French words for a contact button. Easiest of course is the French word *contact*. You might also see the words *nous joindre, nous contacter*, or *nous écrire*, loosely translated as "contact us" or "write to us." Finally, if the site offers a database, you're going to want to search it. Look for a button with the words *recherche* or *rechercher* (Figure D-1).

Society Terms

If your search brings you to a website for a genealogy society or a family surname society, there are other common links that you will find (Figure D-2). If you want to see what's new on the site since the last time you visited it, look for words like *nouveautés, actualités, communiqués*, or *nouvelles* for news.

If you're interested in joining the society, look for *devenir membre* to become a member. Once you've paid your dues, you're going to want access to the "members only" section. Look for *accès aux membres*. To login, look for *connexion*. Then you're going to want to enter your *identifiant* (username) and *mot de passe* (password). If you're like most of us, there's a good chance you will at some point forget your username or password. In that case, look for *identifiant oublié?* and *mot de passe oublié?*

Many societies publish wonderful materials. To see what your society has, look for the tab called *publications*. If you see something you want to purchase, add it to your basket by clicking on *ajouter au panier*. When you're done shopping, then proceed to your *panier d'achat*, or "shopping cart," to check out.

Repository Terms

Another type of French site you might visit is a records repository, such as a library or archives.

Genealogy or Family Society Website Terms	
nouveautés	news
actualités	news
communiqués	news
nouvelles	news
devenir membre	become a member
accès aux membres	members' section
connexion	login
identifiant	username
mot de passe	password
identifiant oublié?	forgot your username?
mot de passe oublié?	forgot your password?
publications	publications
ajouter au panier	add to basket
panier d'achat	shopping cart

Figure D-2: Genealogy/family society website terms

We all know the gold mine of information they hold. But accessing it is a different story if you can't read French.

Perhaps you're looking for information regarding the organization's library, or *bibliothèque*, or perhaps instead it's a digital library, or *bibliothèque numérisée*. Perhaps you're looking for the repository's catalog, or *catalogue*. If you want the link to a particular database, look for a tab or a button that says *bases de donnés*. If it's a site like the PRDH or LaFrance where you need a subscription in order to use it, look for a link to *abonnement* (Figure D-3).

Once you are in the area of the website with all the genealogy data, or *données généalogiques*, you need to navigate through the

Repository Website Terms

bibliothèque	library
bibliothèque numérisée	digital library
catalogue	catalog
bases de donnés	databases
abonnement	subscribe
données généalogiques	genealogy data
précédent	previous
suivant	next
début	beginning
fin	end
nom de famille	surname
prénom	given name
liste alphabétique	alphabetical list
nom	name
naissance	birth
lieu	place
décès	death
âge	age
mariage	marriage
époux/épouse	husband/wife

Figure D-3: Repository website terms

pages. To go back to a previous page, click *précédent*. To move forward, click *suivant*. To jump to the beginning, look for the word *début*, and jump to the end by clicking *fin*.

If a search box appears, it might ask first for you to enter the *nom de famille*, or surname, followed by the *prénom*, or first name. You then might see an alphabetical list, or *liste alphabétique*. Once you know what information is in each column, the rest is easy. Common column headings are *nom* (name), *naissance* (birth), *lieu* (place), *décès* (death), *âge* (age), *mariage* (marriage), and *époux* or *épouse* (spouse).

Consider printing these tables to keep beside your computer.

Appendix E: Typing French Diacritical Marks

While researching your French families, you will come across names, places, and words that contain diacritical marks. These are crucial to the spelling of the word. You will find four different marks for vowels and one for a consonant.

Accent aigu	é
Accent grave	à è ù
Accent circonflexe	â ê î ô û
Tréma	ë
Cédille	ç

You're probably most familiar with the *accent aigu*, which looks like an apostrophe on top of the letter *e*. If you slant the apostrophe in the opposite direction and put it on top of an *a*, *e*, or *u*, you have an *accent grave*. The one that looks like an upside down *V* on top of any of the vowels is called an *accent circonflexe*. It indicates that in Old French, the word was written with an *s* after the vowel. When you have two vowels together and each one makes its own sound, like in the name Noël, the second vowel will have two dots on top of it. This is called a *tréma*.

The only consonant with a diacritical mark is the *c*. It has a dangling tail hanging from the bottom. This is called a *cédille*. It causes the *c* to make an /s/ sound.

In the French language, omitting or misusing these marks is the same as misspelling a word. When transcribing a French document or entering names, places, and words into your genealogy program, how can you easily type the correct letters?

You have several choices. We'll cover two here. If you're going to be doing extensive typing in French to the exclusion of English, you can install a virtual French keyboard. If you're basically typing in English and you just have to occasionally insert accented letters, then you can keep your English keyboard and simply use a quick shortcut to enter these letters. Let's take a look at the virtual keyboard first.

Virtual French Keyboard

For Mac users, search for instructions for installing and using an international keyboard. Use the following steps to set up a French language virtual keyboard in Windows 10.

Right-click the Start Menu (the Windows icon in the bottom left corner of the task bar).
Click Settings.
Click Time & language.
Click Language.

Under Preferred languages, click the plus sign in front of "Add a preferred language" (Figure E-1). In the drop-down box, scroll down to "Français (Canada)." Install the language pack.

Preferred languages

Apps and websites will appear in the first language in the list that they support. Select a language and then select Options to configure keyboards and other features.

+   Add a preferred language

English (United States)
Default app language; Default input language
Windows display language

Français (Canada)
Language pack installed

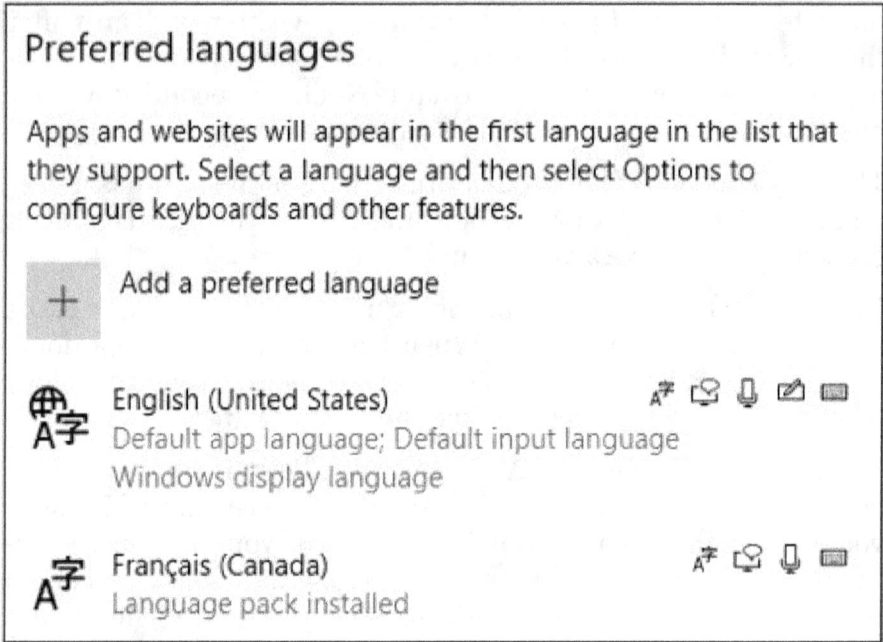

Figure E-1: Settings to install Français (Canada) keyboard

You can change to the French keyboard in two different ways. First, hold down the Windows key and press the spacebar. Or look in the system tray to the right of the task bar (Figure E-2). Here you'll see ENG for English. Click on that and switch to FRA for French.

Figure E-2: Switch to French-Canadian keyboard from the system tray

The three most common accented or diacritical French letters are the é, è, and ç. Once you have installed your virtual French keyboard in Windows 10, switch from ENG to FRA in the system tray. To type an é, tap the forward slash key. For the è, tap the apostrophe key; for the ç tap the end bracket key. For capital letters, just hold down the shift key.

Click on FRA to switch back to the English keyboard again.

Shortcut Keys

I personally prefer this second method, using shortcuts. Since you only need to use a handful of them regularly, it's easy to memorize the codes.

On a PC, you type an accented letter by holding down the ALT key as you type in a specific set of numbers. For example, to type é, you would hold down the ALT key as you type "130." See Figure E-3 for a list of ALT codes for French characters, including the ligatures æ and œ. You might want to print a copy of the table and tape it to the side of your computer monitor for quick access.

The following instructions for a Mac worked during the writing of this book. If the procedure has changed, search online for updated instructions.

For a Mac, you need to hold down the Option key plus a second key simultaneously (Figure E-4). That second key determines the accent mark.

Small letters		Capital letters	
For this letter...	...hold the ALT key and type	For this letter...	...hold the ALT key and type
à	133	À	0192
â	131	Â	0194
ä	132	Ä	0196
æ	145	Æ	0198
ç	135	Ç	0199
é	130	É	0201
è	138	È	0200
ê	136	Ê	0202
ë	137	Ë	0203
î	140	Î	0206
ï	139	Ï	0207
ô	147	Ô	0212
œ	0156	Œ	0140
ù	151	Ù	0217
û	150	Û	0219
ü	129	Ü	0220
«	174	»	175
€	0128		

Figure E-3: Shortcut keys

Then you release both keys and type the letter that you want accented. The ` key (found before the "1" key under the tilde) produces the *accent grave*. The "I" key produces the *accent circonflexe*. Type a "U" for the *tréma* and an "E" for the *accent aigu*. For the *cédille*, hold the Option key and "c" for a small *cédille*, and Shift+Option+c for a capital *cédille*.

Small letters		Capital letters	
For this letter...	...hold the first two keys simultaneously, release, then type letter	For this letter...	...hold the first two keys simultaneously, release, then type letter
á	Option + ´, a	Á	Option + ´, A
à	Option + I, a	À	Option + I, A
ã	Option + U, a	Ã	Option + U, A
æ	Option + '	Æ	Shift + Option + '
ç	Option + c	Ç	Shift + Option + C
é	Option + E, e	É	Option + E, E
è	Option + ´, e	È	Option + ´, E
ê	Option + I, e	Ê	Option + I, E
ë	Option + U, e	Ë	Option + U, E
í	Option + I, i	Í	Option + I, I
ï	Option + U, i	Ï	Option + U, I
ó	Option + I, o	Ó	Option + I, O
œ	Option + q	Œ	Shift + Option + Q
ù	Option + ´, u	Ù	Option + ´, U
û	Option + I, u	Û	Option + I, U
ü	Option + U, u	Ü	Option + U, U

Figure E-4: Shortcut keys on a Mac

Mobile Devices

To type an accented letter on most mobile devices, it is a simple process (Figure E-5). On the screen, just hold your finger on the unaccented letter. A pop-up will give you all possible accents for that letter. Without lifting your finger, drag it to the accented letter you want and release.

Figure E-5: Shortcut keys on mobile devices

Appendix F: Christmas Words

Chronology of Christmas in Québec[68]

1641: The First Nations celebrated Christmas. Father Brébeuf composed a Christmas carol (*chant de Noël*) for the Huron Indians called *Jesous Ahatonhia*, or "Jesus is born." In this story, Father Brébeuf adapted a few items to fit into the native culture: Jesus lay in a lodge of broken bark wrapped in rabbit skins. Hunters (instead of Wise Men) offered fur pelts as gifts.

1645: Early pioneers celebrated Christmas by attending Midnight Mass (*messe de minuit*). They sang Christmas carols (*chants de Noël*) brought over from France and watched the procession of the Christ child to the manger (*crèche*).

---

[68] From the *Canadian Encyclopedia*

1781: North America's first Christmas tree (*l'arbre de Noël* or *le sapin de Noël*) was decorated with fruits and lit with white candles in the home of the Baroness Riedesel in Sorel, Quèbec.

Early 1800s: Christmas was hardly celebrated.

1870s: For the English Canadians and the upper class of French Canadians, Christmas became more secularized.

Late 1800s into early 1900s: Christmas takes on the appearance we are familiar with today. It is a blend of French, English, American, and other influences.

Christmas Words	
chant de Noël	Christmas carol
messe de minuit	midnight mass
crèche	manger
l'arbre de Noël or le sapin de Noël	Christmas tree
réveillon	Christmas feast
tourtière	French-Canadian meat pie
bûche de Noël	Yule log
Papa Noël or Père Noël	Santa Claus
Joyeux Noël	Merry Christmas
Bonne Année	Happy New Year

Figure F-1 : Christmas words

Today the season counts Christmas markets, choirs, and horse-drawn sleigh rides as festive entertainment. After midnight mass (*messe de minuit*) on Christmas eve, families return home for the Christmas feast (*réveillon*) to break their fast. The feast most likely includes some variety of the French-Canadian meat pie (*tourtière*) as well as a Yule log (*bûche de Noël*). Everyone awaits the visit of Santa Claus (*Papa Noël* or *Père Noël*), and on Christmas Day, they enjoy visiting with families and friends (Figure F-1).

Appendix G: Money Words

For good or bad, money plays a huge role in our lives today. Imagine what your life would be like if you didn't physically have any. Imagine what life would be like if our government didn't have any. Our ancestors faced that very situation several times during the colonial period.

Before we take a look at the changing face of money in the colony from the beginning of New France until the conquest, let's learn some of the money terms you may find in such notary records as marriage contracts, sales, or apprenticeships.

In the beginning, the colonists traded, or bartered, with the Natives. But fairly soon, coins were brought into the colony. You're probably familiar with the *sou* (also spelled *sol*) and the *livre*. The *sou* was a French penny. You could divide a *sou* into twelve *deniers*. The word *denier* came from the *denarius*, a ubiquitous Roman coin.

The abbreviation for *livres* is *ll*; *s* for *sous*, and *d* for *denier* (Figure G-1).

Monetary Abbreviations	
8 livres	8ˡˡ
10 sous	10ˢ
5 deniers	5ᵈ

Figure G-1: Monetary abbreviations

Twenty *sous* were equivalent to a *livre*. So there were twelve *deniers* to a *sou*, and twenty *sous* to a *livre*. A *livre* was simply an accounting value. There was no issued denomination worth one *livre*. But other coins could add up to that amount. The *livre* in Canada was referred to as a *livre tournois*, minted in the Touraine region of France, and was comparable to an English pound (Figure G-2). Three *livres tournois* equaled one *écu*. Three *deniers* equaled one *liard*.

English/French Monetary Comparison		
ENGLAND	12 pence = 1 shilling	20 shillings = 1 pound
FRANCE	12 deniers = 1 sou (sol)	20 sous (sols) = 1 livre
1 livre = approximately 1 pound		

Figure G-2: English/French monetary comparison

In the earliest days of Québec, there was a need for low-denomination coins, so France sent large amounts of *double tournois* equal to two *deniers*. Another coin found in the colony was the *louis d'or*, which was worth ten *livres* in 1640 and fifty-four *livres* by 1720.

In *Champlain's Dream*[69] by David Hackett Fischer, he includes the most common coins found in New France and their equivalencies (Figure G-3). These coins were made from copper; silver; gold; and *billon*, a base alloy of tin, copper, and silver.

---

[69] David Hackett Fischer, *Champlain's Dream* (New York: Simon & Schuster, 2008), 632–633

French Coins and Values

Metal	French Coin	Value
Billon	douzain	12 *deniers*
Copper	double tournois	2 *deniers* (4 *deniers* in New France)
	liard	3 *deniers*
	demi-sou	6 *deniers*
	sou	12 *deniers*
	douzain	12 *deniers* (revalued to 15 in 1640)
	deux sols	24 *deniers*
Silver	mousquetaire	20 *deniers*
	quatre sols	32 *deniers*
	six sols	48 *deniers*
	douze sols	96 *deniers*; 1/10 *écu*
	vingt-quatre sols	192 *deniers*; 1/5 *écu*
	petit écu or half écu blanc	½ crown, 5 shillings
Gold	demi-Louis d'or	approximately 3 *écus*
	Louis d'or	a little more than 6 *écus*

Figure G-3: French coins and values

Appendix H: Measurement Words

It is very difficult to present a nice, neat, tidy chart of measurements that were used in France and Nouvelle France. First, the standards upon which these measurements were based were variable: for example, the *pied-de-roi*, or the "foot of the king." Originally, producers must have loved it when the king had small feet, and consumers must have adored their large-footed sovereign. Definitions for these measurements were vague, and people from the various provinces interpreted them differently.

Only the measurements of Paris were used in New France in an attempt to standardize them, and yet there were still variations.

Linear measurement was based on two *graines d'orge*, or two "grains of barley" which equaled one *ligne*. Twelve *lignes* equaled one *pouce*. Twelve *pouces* equaled one *pied-de-roi*, or a foot. Six *pieds* were a *toise*, or a fathom. Three *toises* equaled one *perche*, or perch. Ten *perches* equaled one *arpent*, and eighty-four *arpents* equaled one *lieue*, or league (Figure H-1).

None of that makes any sense until we start comparing it to something we're familiar with. So let's start with the *pied-de-roi*, or foot. In New France, the foot was a bit bigger than we're used to, or 12.789 inches. A typical medium-sized house in Québec in 1670 was about 654 square *pieds*, or about 697 square feet in English measurement, about two-thirds the size of a basic ranch house today.

Linear Measurement			
French Measurement	**=**	**French Measurement**	**Approxiamte English Equivalent**
2 graines d'orge (2 grains of barley)	=	1 ligne	
12 lignes	=	1 pouce	1 inch
12 pouces	=	1 pied-de-roi	1 foot
6 pieds	=	1 toise	1 fathom
3 toises	=	1 perche	1 perch
10 perches	=	1 arpent	length, not area
84 arpents	=	1 lieu	2 leagues

Figure H-1: French linear measurement

If there are twelve *pouces* to a *pied*, each *pouce* is a bit bigger than an inch. In the 1600s when it was standardized, a *pouce* was 1.06575 English inches, literally the size of the king's big toe.

There were several different types of *perches*, but the *perche de Paris* was 19.1835 English feet or 5.847 meters.

An *arpent*, a land measurement commonly found in Canadian records, was both a linear and an area measurement. For distance, it was equal to about 192 English feet, or 58.47 meters. Your ancestral farmer's land would have been measured in the area measurement for *arpents*, which was about 5/6 the size of an English acre.

If there are any sailors in your ancestral family, the *lieue marine*, or nautical league (and there are different types), was 3.45 English miles.

Those are the most common measurements you're likely to run into in the records. There are many more divisions of measurement for distance, area, volume, weight, and depth. If you find a document with a rarer unit of measurement, consult David Hackett Fischer's *Champlain's Deam* or Marcel Trudel's *Introduction to New France.*

Appendix I: Occupation Words

This list is courtesy of the American-Canadian Genealogical Society of Manchester, NH. Merci, beaucoup! The endings in parentheses are the feminine form of the occupation.

FRENCH		ENGLISH
A la retraite	**A**	Retired
Agriculteur		Farmer, husbandman
Aide de sous commis		Helper to asst. clerk
Apothicaire		Pharmacist
Apprenti(e)		Apprentice
Apprêteur (euse)		Tanner/dresser of skins
Archer		Bowman
Architecte		Architect
Argentier		Silversmith
Armurier		Gunsmith
Arpenteur		Land Surveyor
Arquebusier		Matchlock gunsmith
Artisan(e)		Handicraftsman

Aubergiste	**A**	Innkeeper
Aumonier		Army chaplain
Avocat		Lawyer
Bailli	**B**	Bailiff
Banquier (ère)		Money agent, banker
Becheur (euse)		Digger
Bedeau		Church caretaker
Beurrier (ère)		Butter-maker
Bibliothécaire		Librarian
Blanchisseur (eusse)		Laundryman/woman
Bonnetier (ère)		Hosier
Boucher (ère)		Butcher
Boulanger (ère)		Baker
Bourgeois(e)		Business or a privileged person
Boutonnier		Button-maker
Braconnier		Poacher
Brasseur (euse)		Brewer
Briqueteur		Bricklayer
Briquetier		Brick-maker
Bucheron		Woodcutter
Cabaretier (ère)	**C**	Saloon Keeper
Calfat		Caulker
Camionneur		Truck driver
Cannonier		Gunner (cannon)
Cantinier (ère)		Canteen-keeper
Capitaine de milice		Captain of the militia
Capitaine de navire		Ship captain
Capitaine de port		Port captain
Capitaine de vaisseau		Ship captain
Capitaine des troupes		Troup captain
Cardeur (euse)		Carder (textile mill)
Chamoisseur		Chamois-dresser
Chancelier		Chancellor
Chandelier		Candle-maker
Chanteur (euse)		Singer
Chapelier (ère)		Hatter

	C	
Charbonnier (ere)		Coal Merchant
Charcutier (ère)		Pork-butcher
Charpentier		Carpenter
Charpentier de navires		Shipwright
Charretier		Carter
Charron		Cartwright/wheelwright
Chasseur (eresse)		Hunter
Chaudronnier		Coppersmith, tinsmith
Chaufournier		Furnace tender
Chevalier		Horseman, cavalry
Chirurgien		Surgeon
Cloutier		Nail-maker or dealer
Cocher		Coachman, driver
Colonel		Colonel
Commandant		Commander
Commis		Clerk
Commissaire d'artillerie		Arms stewart
Commissaire de la marine		Ship's purser
Compagnon		Journeyman
Comptable		Accountant, book-keeper
Concierge		Janitor, caretaker
Confiseur (euse)		Confectioner
Conseilleur		Counsellor, advisor
Contrebandier		Smuggler
Contremaître		Overseer, foreman
Controleur		Superintendent
Cordier		Rope maker
Cordonnier		Shoemaker/cobbler
Corroyeur		Currier, leather-dresser
Coureur-des-bois		Trapper (runner of the woods)
Courrier		Courier, messenger
Coutelier		Cutlery maker
Couturier (ère)		Tailor, dressmaker
Couvreur		Roofer
Couvreur en ardoise		Slate roofer
Cuisinier (ère)		Cook

Cuisinier en chef	**C**	Head cook (chef)
Cultivateur (trice)		Farmer
Débardeur	**D**	Stevedore
Défricheur		Clearer (of forest)
Dentiste		Dentist
Domestique		Indentured servant, farmhand
Douairière		Dowager
Douanier (ère)		Custom officer
Drapier		Cloth maker, clothier
Ébeniste	**E**	Cabinet-maker
Ecclésiastique		Clergyman
Échevin		Alderman
Écolier (ère)		Student
Écuyer		Esquire
Éleveur (euse)		Breeder (of animals)
Engagé Ouest		Hired to trap furs out west
Enseigne		Ensign
Enseigne de vaisseau		Sub-lieutenant on a ship
Épicier (ère)		Grocer
Esclave		Slave
Farinier	**F**	Flour merchant or miller
Faux-saunier		Dealer in contraband salt
Ferblantier		Tinsmith
Fermier (ère)		Farmer
Ferrant		Farrier, one who shoes horses
Fondeur		Founder, caster
Forgeron		Blacksmith
Fourreur		Furrier
Fraudeur		Defrauder
Fromager (ère)		Cheese-maker
Garde	**G**	Guard, watchman
Garde-magazin		Store-keeper
Garde-malade		Nurse's aid
Gardien (enne)		Guardian, keeper, attendant
Geolier (ère)		Prison guard
Gerant(e)		Manager

Gouverneur Général	**G**	Governor of New France
Greffier		Town clerk/recorder
Greffier de la Justice		Clerk of the Court
Horloger	**H**	Clock-maker
Horticulteur (euse)		Horticulturalist
Hospitalier (ère)		Hospital worker
Hotelier (êre)		Hotel-keeper
Huissier		Process server, usher, bailiff
Huissier audiencier		Court crier
Huissiers		Guardians/caretakers
Imprimeur	**I**	Printer
Infirmière		Nurse
Ingenieur		Engineer
Inspecteur (trice)		Inspector
Intendant		Administrator
Interprète		Interpreter
Jardinier (ère)	**J**	Gardener
Journalier		Day Laborer
Journaliste		Journalist
Juge		Judge
Laboureur	**L**	Farmer, ploughman
Laitier (ère)		Dairyman
Libraire		Bookseller
Lieutenant criminel		Royal magistrate of criminal matters
Lieutenant général et civil		Military rank as division general
Maçon	**M**	Mason
Maître		Master (at his craft)
Maître canonnier		Artilleryman
Maître de barque		Ship master
Maître de poste		Postmaster
Maître d'école		School teacher
Maître d'hotel		Head-waiter
Major (de medecin)		Medical officer
Manoeuvrier		Jack-of-all-trades
Maraicher (ère)		Market gardener

Marbrier	**M**	Marble-cutter
Marchand(e)		Merchant
Marchand de fourrures		Fur merchant/trader
Maréchal-ferrant		Horseshoe smith
Marguiller		Church warden
Marin		Marine
Matelot		Sailor
Mecanicien (enne)		Mechanic, machinist
Médecin		Medical doctor
Mégissier		Leather-dresser
Mendiant(e)		Beggar
Menuisier		Joiner or cabinet maker
Mercier		Haberdasher, dealer in dress maker supplies
Messire		Title of honor or nobility
Meunier (ère)		Miller
Mineur		Minor or miner
Modiste		Milliner
Mouleur		Molder of cast iron
Mousse		Cabin-boy
Musicien (enne)		Musician
Navigateur	**N**	Sailor/navigator
Nettoyeur (euse) de		Cleaner of
Notaire		Notary
Notaire Royal		Notary Appointed by king
Nourrice		Nurse and/or wet nurse
Officier	**O**	Officer
Orfevre		Gold or silversmith
Ouvrier		Workman, laborer
Passeur	**P**	Ferryman
Patissier (ère)		Pastry cook/bakery owner
Peaussier		Skin-dresser
Pêcheur (euse)		Fisherman
Peigneur (euse)		Comber of textiles
Peintre		Painter
Pelletier		Furrier

Percepteur (trice)	**P**	Tax Collector
Perruquier		Wig-maker
Pharmacien (enne)		Druggist
Pilote		Pilot (of ships)
Plombier		Plumber
Pompier		Fireman
Porcher		Swine-keeper
Portefaix		Porter
Portier		Porter/janitor
Postier (ère)		Postal-clerk
Postillon		Coacher (horses)
Potier		Potter
Potier d'étain		Tinsmith and/or Pewtersmith
Précepteur (trice)		Tutor, teacher
Prétre		Priest
Prévote		Military police
Prisonnier		Prisoner
Procureur		Attorney, prosecutor
Procureur Général		Magistrate of the court
Ramoneur	**R**	Chimney-sweep
Receveur des droits		Tax collector
Relieur		Book binder
Religieux (euse)		Priest or nun
Retiré(e)		Retired
Roulier		Wagoner, truck-driver
Sabotier	**S**	Maker of wooden shoes
Sage-femme		Mid-wife
Salinier		Salt-maker or salt merchant
Sans profession		Without occupation
Saunier		Salt-maker
Scieur		Sawyer
Scieur de long		Pit sawyer
Scieur de pierre		Stone-cutter
Sculpteur		Sculptor
Secrétaire		Secretary

Seigneur	**S**	Owner of a fief or a seigneurial estate
Serger		Weaver of serge cloth
Sergetier		Weaver of wool serge
Serrurier		Locksmith
Serviteur		Servant, man-servant
Sieur		Gentleman (same as Esquire)
Soeur		Sister (nun)
Soeur Hospitalière		Sister of Charity – hospital worker
Soldat		Soldier
Sous-commis		Assistant clerk
Subrogé(e)		Deputy, surrogate
Syndic		Trustee
Taillandier	**T**	Edge-tool maker
Tailleur		Taylor
Tailleur de pierres		Stone mason
Tailleur d'habits		Tailor of clothing
Tailleuse		Dressmaker
Tanneur		Tanner
Tapissier (ère)		Upholsterer
Teinturier (ère)		Dyer
Timonier		Helmsman
Tireur-de-laine		Wool-worker
Tisserand(e)		Weaver
Tisserand en drap		Weaver of cloth
Tisserand en sergé		Weaver of serge cloth
Tisserand en serge		Weaver of twill cloth
Tisserand en toile		Weaver of linen
Tisseur (euse)		Weaver
Tondeur		Sheep shearer
Tonnelier		Cooper
Tourneur (euse)		Turner of lathe or potter's wheel
Traitant(e)		Practitioner
Traiteur		Restaurant or inn-keeper
Trappeur		Trapper

Trésorier (ère)		Treasurer
Truchement des sauvages	**T**	Interpreter, go-between
Vacher (ère)	**V**	Cow-keeper
Valet		Valet
Vannier		Basket-maker
Vigneron (onne)		Vine-grower
Vinaigrier		Vinigar-maker or merchant
Vitrier		Glazier
Voilier		Sail-maker
Voiturier (ère)		Carter, carrier
Volontaire		Volunteer
Voyageur		Fur trapper/trader
Voyer		Surveyor of roads

Appendix J:
Given Names in Latin
Records

Not all priests wrote in their parish registers in French. As you search through Quebec baptism, marriage, and burial records, you'll sometimes discover that the priest recorded the information in Latin!

Just as you can learn to pick out information in French records, you can do the same in Latin records. Let's first look at different forms of given names in Latin.

Endings

You determine the precise meaning of a word in Latin by its ending. You add an -s to the end of an English word to indicate plural. In Latin, you add an ending to indicate not only plural, but other cases as well.

The three cases often used in French-Canadian records are the nominative case for the subject, the genitive case for the possessive, and the accusative case for a direct object. A change of ending changes the case and the meaning. To say, "The girl returned," the word for "girl," the subject, is *puella*. In "the book of the girl," "the girl" is possessive, or genitive in Latin, and would be *puellae*. The *-ae* ending indicates possessive. In "I saw the girl," you would use *puellam*, the *-am* ending indicating direct object (accusative). In the baptism record for François Crévier (Figure J-1) from the Cathédrale de l'Assomption in Trois Rivières, all three cases appear.

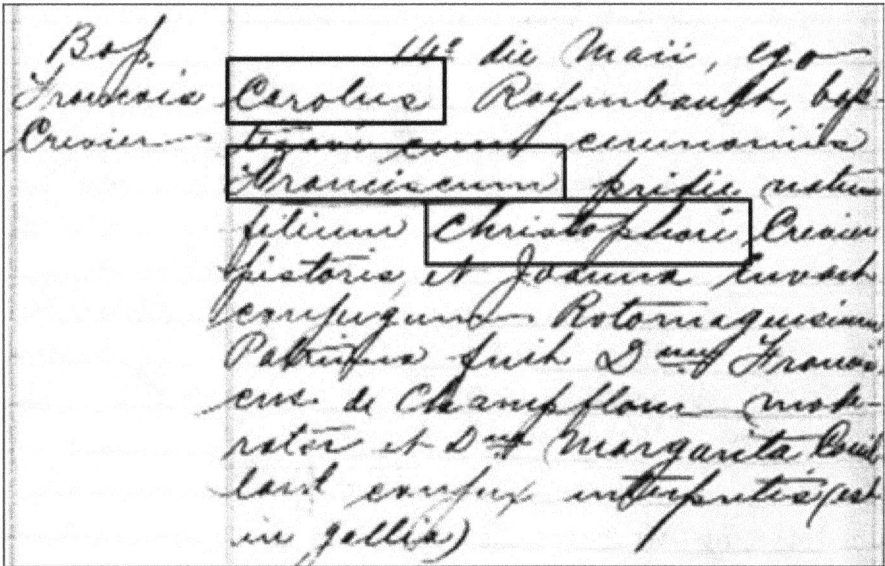

Figure J-1: Latin cases in a baptism record

Declensions

Did you notice that the names in the record above did not end in *-a*, *-ae*, or *-am* like the word *puella* above? That's because nouns belong in one of five declensions in Latin, and each declension has its own set of endings. The word *puella* as well as most female names belong in the first declension. That means all names in the nominative will end in *-a*, the genitive in *-ae*, and the accusative in *-am*. In Latin, the word for Marie is *Maria*. If Maria owns something, you would indicate that by changing the ending on her name to *Mariae*. If her name was the direct object in the sentence, you would write *Mariam*.

Most male names belong to the second declension. Subjects in the nominative case end in *-us*. The genitive ending is *-i*, and the accusative ending is *-um*. In the record above, the priest says, "I [*ego*] *Carolus Raymbault*." He is the subject of the sentence and therefore uses the nominative case for the word Charles. He then says, "I baptized *Franciscum*." Since it's a direct object, *Franciscum* is in the accusative case for 2nd declension nouns. François is the son "of Christophe," so the father's name indicates possession. It is in the genitive case and ends in *-i* (Figure J-2).

Below are tables for common female (Figure J-3) and male (Fig-

Latin Cases in French Records			
Case	**Use**	**Example in Latin**	**In English**
Nominative	Subject	[ego] Carolus Raymbault	[I] Charles Raymbault
Genitive	Possessive	[son of] Christophori	[son of] Christophe
Accusative	Direct object	[I baptised] Franciscum	[I baptised] François

Figure J-2: Latin cases in French records

ure J-4) names written in the nominative, genitive, and accusative cases. Notice that the girl's name *Agnès* and the boys' names, *Jean* and *Michel*, do not follow the same pattern as the others. That's because those names belong to the 3rd declension which, as you can see, has a different set of endings.

If you want to practice on some actual 17th-century records in Latin, check out the parishes of Laprairie, l'Ancienne Lorette, and Trois Rivières.

French Name *=3rd declension	Nominative (Subject)	Genitive (Possessive)	Accusative (Direct Object)
Agnès	Agneta*	Agnetis	Agnetem
Alice	Alicia	Aliciae	Aliciam
Angèle	Angela	Angelae	Angelam
Angélique	Angélica	Angélicae	Angélicam
Anne	Anna	Annae	Annam
Catherine	Catherina	Catherinae	Catherinam
Charlotte	Carola	Carolae	Carolam
Claire	Clara	Clarae	Claram
Denise	Dionysia	Dionysiae	Dionysiam
Dorothée	Dorothea	Dorotheae	Dorotheam
Françoise	Francisca	Franciscae	Franciscam
Hélène	Helena	Helenae	Helenam
Jeanne	Joanna	Joannae	Joannam
Joséphine	Josepha, Josephina	Josephae, Josephinae	Josepham, Joséphinam
Louise	Ludovica	Ludovicae	Ludovicam
Marie	Maria	Mariae	Mariam
Marguerite	Marg(u)arita	Margaritae	Margaritam
Renée	Renata	Renatae	Renatam
Philomène	Philomena	Philomenae	Philomenam
Thérèse	Theresia	Theresiae	Theresiam
Sophie	Sophia	Sophiae	Sophiam

Figure J-3: Common female names in Latin

French Name *=3rd declension	Nominative (Subject)	Genitive (Possessive)	Accusative (Direct Object)
Adolphe	Adolphus	Adolphi	Adolphum
Albert	Albertus	Alberti	Albertum
Alexandre	Alexandrus	Alexandri	Alexandrum
Alfred	Alfredus	Alfredi	Alfredum
Alphonse	Alphonsus	Alphonsi	Alphonsum
Antoine	Antonius	Antonii	Antonium
Basile	Basilius	Basilii	Basilium
Bernard	Bernardus	Bernardi	Bernardum
Charles	Carolus	Caroli	Carolum
Cristophe	Christoferus Xtoferus	Christoferi Xtoferi	Christoferum Xtoferum
Denis	Dionysius	Dionysii	Dionysium
Edouard	Edouardus	Edouardi	Edouardum
Etienne	Stephanus	Stephani	Stephanum
Eugène	Eugenius	Eugenii	Eugenium
François	Franciscus	Francisci	Franciscum
Frederick	Fredericus	Frederici	Fredericum
Georges	Georgius	Georgii	Georgium
Gilbert	Gilbertus	Gilberti	Gilbertum
Gilles	Aegidius Egidius	Aegidii Egidii	Aegidium Egidium
Grégoire	Gregorius	Gregorii	Gregorium
Guillaume	Gulielmus	Gulielmi	Gulielmum

Figure J-4: Common male names in Latin, part 1

French Name *=3rd declension	Nominative (Subject)	Genitive (Possessive)	Accusative (Direct Object)
Henri	Henricus	Henrici	Henricum
Jacques	Jacobus	Jacobi	Jacobum
Jean	J[I]ohannes *	Johannis	Johannem
Joseph	Josephus	Josephi	Josephum
Louis	Ludovicus	Ludivici	Ludovicum
Martin	Martinus	Martini	Martinum
Mathieu	Matthaeus	Matthaei	Mattaeum
Maurice	Mauritius	Mauritii	Mauritium
Michel	Michael *	Michaelis	Michealem
Olivier	Oliverus	Oliveri	Oliverum
Paul	Paulus	Pauli	Paulum
Philippe	Philippus	Philippi	Philippum
Pierre	Petrus	Petri	Petrum
Richard	Ricardus	Ricardi	Ricardum
Robert	Robertus	Roberti	Robertum

Figure J-4: Common male names in Latin, part 2

Appendix K:
Latin Baptism, Marriage, and Burial Records

In Appendix J, you learned how to tell the role of a person in a Latin church record. If a name is in the nominative case, the person is the subject of the sentence. If the name is in the genitive case, that person possesses or has or owns something. The named person received the action in the sentence if the name is in the accusative case.

But what kind of record is it? You found your ancestor's name, but is it his baptism, marriage, or burial record?

Let's say you are searching for the baptism record of Joseph Guyon in L'Ancienne Lorette. You discover the records are in Latin. What do you do?

First, check the margin (Figure K-1). Many priests and missionaries wrote *B* or *Bap* for a baptism record and *S*, Sep, or + for a burial record. For marriages, look for a document with two people mentioned in the margin or the word *matrimonio*. Remember that the names may not be what you're expecting. Joseph may be "Josephus." Louise might be recorded as "Ludovica." (See Appendix J for lists of male and female names in Latin.)

If common abbreviations are not used, then you need to look for particular Latin words in either the margin or the record itself.

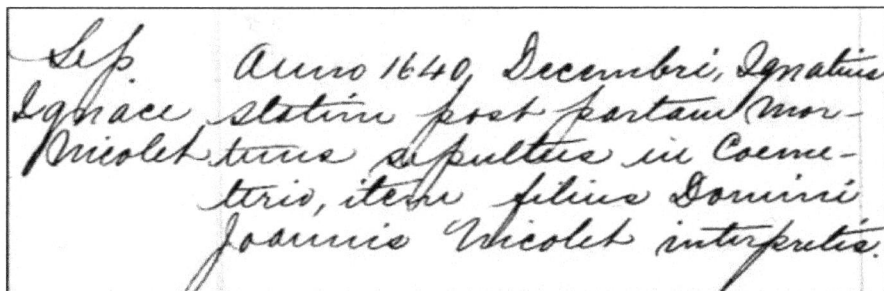

Figure K-1: Burial record in Latin

Baptisms

Latin is a language built on roots. Endings modify the meanings of those roots. So for births, look for the root *nat*. In this record for Margarite Mesnier, notice the word *nata*. The ending indicates a female (Figure K-2).

Figure K-2: Clues in Latin endings

The word *natus* appears in the margin for Ludovicus (Latin for Louis) because -*us* is the male ending (Figure K-3). Both margins also show the abbreviation *bap* or *bapt* for "baptism."

Louis was never called *Ludovicus*. His parents used his French name. The Latin form was only used in official records.

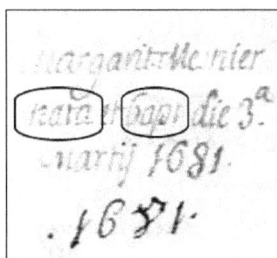

Figure K-3: Clues in Latin endings

Marriages

Look for words or abbreviations similar to *matrimonio, conjuncti, copulatus, ligavi,* or *sponsatus*. These indicate a marriage record.

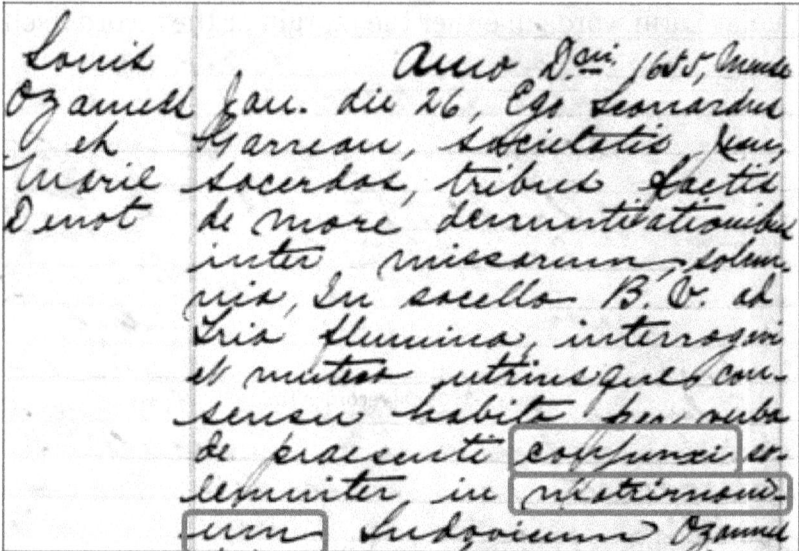

Figure K-4: Marriage clues in Latin records

Burials

In burial records, look for words that contain the following words or roots: *defunct-, mort-, obiit,* or *sep-*.

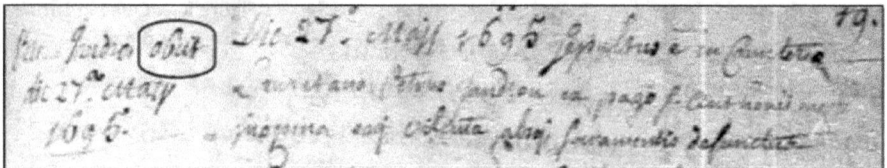

Figure K-5: Burial clues in Latin records

Using What You Learned

Let's go back to the problem presented at the beginning of this chapter. You were hypothetically looking for a baptism record for Joseph Guyon in the registers for L'Ancienne Lorette. You found the following record. Is it what you were looking for? Is it a baptism record? Is it for a child named Joseph Guyon?

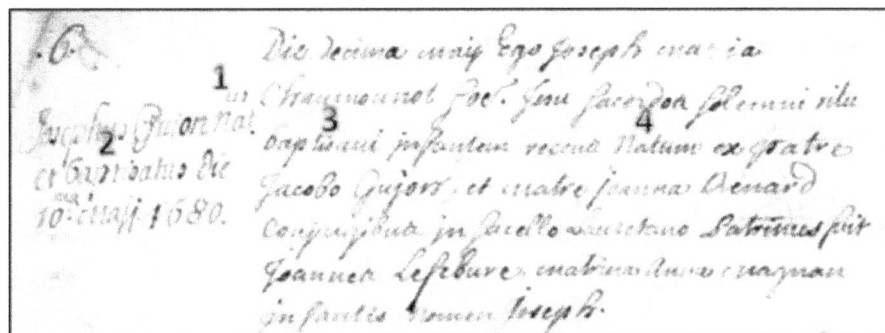

Figure K-6: Mystery record

Let's take a closer look. The name in the margin, Josephus, is the Latin form for Joseph. The letter *y* is often written as an *i* in Latin, so *Guion* is the same surname as *Guyon*.

The margin also contains the word *nat-* (#1) with the rest of the word, -*us*, above it. That indicates that a male child was born. *Baptisatus* (#2) indicates he was baptised. Under the number 3 is the word *baptisavi*, or "I have baptised." Under the #4 is another form of the word "born," *natum*. All these clues indicate that this is a baptism record for Joseph Guyon.

More Resources

FamilySearch.org has an online course called Key Words and Phrases in Latin Records[70] that you might find useful. Its Genealogical Word List [71] includes Latin abbreviations, numbers, months, days of the week, and relationship words, as well as links to more helpful resources.

---

[70] https://www.familysearch.org/ask/learningViewer/68
[71] https://www.familysearch.org/wiki/en/Latin_Genealogical_Word_List

Index

S

T

V

W

www.ingramcontent.com/pod-product-compliance
Lightning Source LLC
Chambersburg PA
HW062200270326
0CB00009B/1594